Minute Sketches of
Great Composers

MINUTE SKETCHES
of
GREAT COMPOSERS

by

EVA vB. HANSL
and
HELEN L. KAUFMANN
With 74 full-page portraits by
SAMUEL NISENSON

GROSSET & DUNLAP
Publishers
NEW YORK

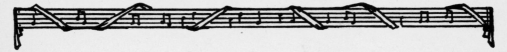

FOREWORD

SELECTING the composers to be included in this volume is like choosing best friends from a large circle, a formidable, not to say delicate undertaking. The stream of music, which started centuries ago as a slender trickle, has become in our time a roaring torrent. The brooks and rivulets which have swelled its volume—in other words, the composers who have made unquestionable contribution to the development of the glorious art of music—will be found between these covers.

Thanks to our Puritan ancestry, which taught us to frown upon the pagan arts of music, painting and the dance, we in America have been heavily handicapped in developing creative powers in those arts. But the symphony concert, the small orchestra, the phonograph and, above all, the radio, have familiarized us increasingly with the good and the great in music, so that we are gradually becoming a nation of appreciative listeners. Some composers are here included because our bowing acquaintance with them through performance of their works has made us wish to know them better.

While these are primarily "lives," every effort has been made to convey the savor of personality as well as the sinew of biography. Furthermore, the thread of historical development is unraveled, so that the book should stand, not only as another reference volume, but one that bears reading as a story of the continuous growth of music.

We have made our classification in the broadest possible way, since there are actually no hard and fast lines between the different schools and periods, and since many composers have written in two or three styles. There will be an attempt to make only the most obvious distinctions between the four large groups:—Classic; romantic (including program); operatic; and modern.

The earliest music on which all these were based was, naturally, as pious and god-fearing as the people for whom it was written and the life of the day in which it was conceived. It consisted of pure and single-line chants that could be sung in the churches by rote and without note. Upon it was built the polyphonic or many-voiced writing of Bach. Handel, Haydn, and Mozart, together with the other classicists, stood for the absolute in music, for the gold of beauty-for-its-own-sake, unalloyed by the dross of personal emotion. With all their sense of harmony of blended tones and of limpid melody, they retained in their writing a detachment and a purity which distinguished it from what preceded and what followed.

The giant Beethoven was the first one actually to break away into the expression in music of his own personal feelings. In some of his works he followed the classical forms; in others he evolved new forms in which to express his emotional inner life, so that he is regarded as the great bridge from the classic to the romantic composers. Schumann, Schubert, Chopin, Brahms were all of that romantic group to whom the music they wrote was a sort of confessional in which they bared to the public gaze their private yearnings and strivings. The advent of program music, wherein the composer provided compositions with elaborate notes telling the story thereof, accompanied and supplemented the development of the romantic school.

Early church music became secularized in two ways, instrumentally and in song. The development of opera was the result of the latter—a development that ran parallel with that of instrumental music, unfolding slowly from the *opéra bouffe* and *opéra comique* of early days, through the trying period when florid Italian coloratura was all the rage, to the refined and refreshing simplicity of Gluck and thence, step by step, to the dramatic fire and orchestral grandeur that was Wagner and the fairy elusiveness that was Debussy. Almost every composer tried his hand at an opera or two, but only those who made it their chief musical preoccupation are here included among opera composers.

Those who are "the moderns," to-day, express the storm and stress of twentieth century living as fervently as the romantics their personal pains and pleasures. They have voiced their impressions in terms so suitable to their subject that sometimes they are quite at variance with accepted ideas of melody, harmony, counterpoint and form. They are for stern reality, without disguise or evasion. As one composer remarked, "You cannot express open wounds with pretty noises," but that consideration has not deterred present-day composers from trying to express open wounds! Every aspect of life is game for the modern musical huntsman, so long as it signifies reality.

If anyone's favorite composer has been omitted from these pages, the authors' apologies are humbly proffered, with the reminder that limitations of space cannot be evaded, but that, under sufficient persuasion, another volume might be forthcoming, wherein all such stepchildren would receive due recognition.

H. L. K.

CONTENTS

"THERE IS MUSIC IN THE AIR; MUSIC ALL AROUND US.
THE WORLD IS FULL OF IT, AND YOU SIMPLY TAKE AS
MUCH AS YOU REQUIRE."

—*Sir Edward Elgar*

Giovanni Pierluigi da Palestrina

"PRINCEPS MUSICAE"

[Born 1525—Died 1594]

God's in His Heaven, all's right with the world" is what young Giovanni Pierluigi might have sung one bright Spring day about 1538, as he passed by the church of Santa Maria Maggiore in Rome, whither he had repaired for a day's outing from his home town of Palestrina. So clearly and joyously did he sing that the priest at his orisons in the church promptly invited him to become a choir-boy there, an invitation he as promptly accepted. Later he became organist of the little church of San Agapito in Palestrina [from which he took his name] until he was summoned to Rome, and all the rest of his curiously quiet and uneventful life was passed in writing music for the church and training choirs to sing it.

He was wholly dependent for his livelihood upon the favor of the reigning pope. Thus his first book of masses was fulsomely dedicated to Pope Julius, a kindly patron, while the glorious *Mass of Marcellus*, tendered Julius' successor, was one of his finest. But Paul, his successor, was a sour soul, who banished Palestrina from the choir because married choir-masters were displeasing to Mother Church. So at the height of his powers Palestrina was obliged to retire to poverty, illness, the wife he had married at twenty-one, and their two children.

In a few months, however, another church sought him out, and rightly. Church music had been in a bad way. The songs of the streets had invaded its purity and vulgarized the church service, and an august committee, the Council of Trent, having been in session for twenty years trying to determine what should be done about it, now proclaimed that the masses of Palestrina, being the only ones which wholly embodied their ideal of pure music, should be used as models. No wonder his townspeople gave him a great demonstration when he was fifty, as they marched through the streets of Rome, Palestrina at their head, singing in chorus the music he had written.

That music was perfect of its kind. He took the cantus firmus, or simple theme, and wrote two or three harmonizing voices of the utmost candor to be sung with it. This laid the foundation for later polyphonic, or many-voiced writing. Without a Palestrina there might have been no Bach, no Beethoven. The title *Princeps Musicae*, graven on his tomb in Rome, where he died February 2, 1594, marked him as the first prince of a royal lineage of church composers.

William Byrd

"MASTER OF THE MADRIGAL"
[Born 1538—Died 1623]

*I*N THE days of good Queen Elizabeth, there were no concerts. Music was a social pastime for the home. The resourceful hostess passed out parts of songs after dinner as casually as she deals a hand of bridge to-day. Byrd wrote, "Since singing is so good a thing, I wish all men would learn to sing." And all the educated ones did read and sing at sight, so that a new song was hailed more eagerly than a new jazz piece to-day.

William Byrd, lovingly dubbed "Father of Musicke," was the pioneer among English composers of Elizabeth's day, and contributed largely, not only to these dinner-party concerts, but to church and instrumental music as well. Born in Lincolnshire in 1538, and "bred up to musicke under Thomas Tallis," he became organist of Lincoln Cathedral at twenty. A year later he married, and five or six children duly appeared. He became a county gentleman, though he had to win many lawsuits in order to retain his property. But he emerged victorious, with an estate at Stondon Place, a coat of arms and an annuity from the Crown. The annuity was granted him after the monopoly on printing and selling music and music-paper graciously accorded to him and Tallis in 1575, proved to be an empty, unremunerative honor.

The accounts of his life are incomplete, but we know that he lived piously but energetically to the ripe age of eighty, despite the fact that for fifteen years before his death he kept alluding in melancholy strain to its imminence. Many great nobles were his patrons, and their support overcame the petty persecutions he suffered as a Papist under a Protestant Queen. He prayed that he might live and die a "true and perfect member of the holy Catholic church," and his prayer was granted.

There are eight published volumes of his works, including motets for the church, madrigals, and pieces composed for Queen Elizabeth's virginal, the ancestor of our piano. It is safe to say that his book of Psalms, Sonnets and Songs marked the beginning of the Golden Age of English music, and that his madrigals made England a "nest of singing birds." Certainly he richly earned the dedication in a book of songs by one of his pupils, "To William Byrd, a Great Maister of Musicke, which for skill and sweetness may content the most curious."

H. Purcell.

Henry Purcell

"THE FATHER OF ENGLISH SONG"

[*Born 1658—Died 1695*]

A JOVIAL King Cole who relished his pipe and his bowl of an evening at a cozy inn, and who wrote many songs for his fiddlers three, expressing frolicsome, as well as more serious moods, Henry Purcell and his music live to-day as the essence of the Elizabethan era, when the world, the flesh and the devil throve side by side with the church and its ministers.

Little St. Anne's Lane, Old Pye Street, Westminster,—thus melodiously was yclept the scene of his birth in 1658. His father, a "singing man of Westminster Abbey," having died when Henry was but six, his uncle Thomas became the sympathetic guardian of the boy and his musical talents.

In his youth, as chorister of the Chapel Royal, he learned from Humfrey, Master of the Children, not only the old Gregorian chants, but the newer idiom of the Italians and the Frenchman, Lully. At the same time, he became an accomplished organist and, later, when his voice broke, music copyist in Westminster Abbey.

When James II was crowned with pomp and ceremony, Henry, in his capacity of organist of the Abbey, an honor bestowed when he was but twenty-two, superintended the erection of a new organ for the event. The prize-money he received inspired him to compose two fine anthems: "*My Heart Is Inditing*" and "*I Was Glad*"; also an ode "*Why are All the Muses Mute?*" Yet, several years later, when James was in disgrace, Purcell's comic song *Lilliebullero* helped to ridicule him out of three kingdoms.

His twenty adult years were crowded with enduring work of four types— Sacred Music, Odes and Welcome Songs, Music for Amateurs, and Dramatic Music. *Dido and Aenaeas*, written in 1680 for performance by "the young gentlewomen of Mr. Josiah Priest's school at Chelsea," the four-part chorus "*In these Delightful, Pleasant Groves*," and the Shakespeare song, "*Come Unto these Yellow Sands*" are frequently sung.

He died, appropriately, on the eve of that St. Cecilia's Day, November 21, 1695, which he had celebrated in his greatest Ode, the *Ode to St. Cecilia*. The anthems, "*Blessed is the Man that Fears the Lord*" and "*Thou Knoweth, Lord, the Secrets of Our Hearts*," composed by him for the funeral of Queen Mary six months previously, solemnized his own impressive obsequies in the Abbey. He shares with Byrd the title of "Father of English Song."

Jean Baptiste Lully

"MUSICAL DICTATOR OF 17th CENTURY FRANCE"

[*Born 1633—Died 1687*]

THE life of Jean Baptiste Lully kaleidoscopes into a series of brilliant images. We see him first, a monkey-faced little Italian boy, born in Florence of poor parents in 1633, and there picked up by the Duc de Guise, to be carried as a gift to Mlle. de Montpensier in Paris. He is the pet of the household for awhile, but soon is relegated to the kitchen in favor of a new toy, where he solaces himself by giving impromptu concerts. His song, "*Au Clair de la Lune*" is said to have caused a long wait between entrée and roast. Mademoiselle, hearing of his talent, has him taught music, and dresses him in the peruke of her orchestra.

At nineteen his service with her is terminated by his song lampooning her, but his lifetime friendship with Louis XIV, "le Roi Soleil," begins. He rises rapidly from a mere violinist in the King's orchestra to director of a special band. Every player must learn to read at sight, and the director's sharp-tongued exactions bring his orchestra close to perfection.

Louis is delighted with Lully, who "dances divinely," acts the clown in Molière comedies, plays violin and spinet, writes ballets. He loads him with honors accorded only to noblemen, winks at his dissipations and impertinences, gives him handsome presents when he marries and produces six children.

In 1672, Lully steps out as opera composer and master of ceremonies at Louis' Grandes Fêtes at Versailles. He writes an opera a year from now until his death, in 1687. In candle-lit gardens, where fountains play and banquet-tables groan under rare viands, the monarch and his court graciously view *Alceste*, *Cadmus et Hermione*, and *Roland*. *Atys*, "l'opéra du Roi," *Isis*, "l'opéra des Musiciens," *Phaeton*, "l'opéra du Peuple," please all tastes. The song, "*Amour, Que Veux-tu de Moi*" is sung throughout the kingdom. The productions are of a lavishness that puts present-day productions to shame. Women replace men in the ballets. Overtures introducing the operas are an innovation, bringing out new orchestral effects which later composers seize upon.

An untidy little man, peering with red-lidded eyes at the harpsichord keys, upon which he drops snuff while composing; a lion raging at the greatest poets of the day, because their lines do not match his inspiration; a dictator taking tribute from his musical subjects; a perfect son of the "grand siècle," whose influence, if not his music, lives on,—such is Lully.

Couperin.

François Couperin
"COURT MUSICIAN TO LOUIS XIV"
[Born 1668—Died 1733]

A COAT of arms consisting of a sky-blue ground, silver stars, a golden sun, and a golden lyre rewarded Couperin's labors for His Majesty Louis XIV, and its delicate pastel coloring seems perfectly to express the exquisite quality of his music.

He was the last of a long family lineage of musicians, to whose supposedly superior merit he paid modest tribute, although in reality his genius vastly exceeded theirs. Paris was his birthplace, and in or near Paris he made his home from his birth on November 10, 1668, until his death in 1733.

Maitre Thomelin, an organ virtuoso of much local renown and an intimate family friend, gave him such an excellent musical training that the pupil replaced the master as court organist upon the latter's death. This was no small honor, for his August Majesty himself supervised the competition, and made the final selection of young François from a large number of contestants.

In 1694, Couperin, already a married man of five years' standing, assumed the honorable title of "Maitre de Clavecin des Enfants de France," and taught all the younger generation of Royalty to tinkle prettily upon the harpsichord, in addition to fulfilling his duties as organist and composer of pieces for all the festivities of a pleasure-loving Court.

About this time, some trios of the Italian, Corelli, were played at a musicale, whose brilliancy enthralled the volatile French audience. At the first opportunity, the canny Couperin had some of his own compositions performed, which he wrote in the same brilliant style, and signed with an Italian version of his own name,—Pernucio. It was not until long afterward that he confessed the innocent deception; meanwhile, thanks largely to him, the Italian influence had come to stay.

There were no music publishers then, but he himself brought out four large folio volumes of pieces for the harpsichord, done on copper-plate, a magnificent example of bookmaking. His little pieces,—*Allemandes*, *Courantes*, *Sarabandes*, *Gigues*, *Rondos*,—were perfect in form, and tinkle as melodiously now as in their own day. He made harpsichord music as expressive as it can possibly be made. His larger works,—*La Pucelle*, *La Sultane*, *La Steinquerque*, all written for special court occasions, are seldom played, but the seven *Sonates à Trois* and the harpsichord pieces are classic.

Delicate in health, as in his work, he died in 1733 at sixty-five, leaving trailing wisps of fragile but deathless melody to support his fame.

Rameau

Jean Philippe Rameau

"COMPOSITEUR DE LA MUSIQUE DE LA CHAMBRE"

[Born 1683—Died 1764]

*H*IS contemporaries probably called him "the old grouch," for he appears to have been a close-fisted, unamiable and inarticulate old gentleman, although at forty-three he won a bride of eighteen —surely enough to have sweetened his sour disposition.

His father, organist of the cathedral in Dijon, sat him down before a harpsichord as soon after his birth (September 25, 1683) as his baby fingers would function. His musical education prepared him so well for the study of law, that he persisted in scribbling music in all his note-books and singing aloud in the class-room, a practice which procured summary curtailment of his legal career.

A passion for a young widow at seventeen sent him packing off to Italy, to the improvement of his epistolary style and the enrichment of his musical life. He spent some time in Paris; then, disgruntled by his failure to secure a competitive post as organist there, he withdrew to the mountains of Auvergne.

From the experimental studies of that retirement came his *Treatise on Harmony Reduced to its Natural Principles*, the foundation of a new philosophic science of harmony which he followed with other learned writings on the same subject.

Nevertheless, until after his fortieth year he was comparatively unknown. His ambition to write operas went begging until a musical Maecenas of Paris introduced him to Abbé Pellegrin, who wrote the book for *Hypolite et Aricie* and was so charmed with Rameau's music that at its first performance he publicly destroyed the agreement by which Rameau had promised payment in the event of its failure.

From 1745 on a new opera was born each year. *La Princesse de Navarre* (Voltaire, librettist) won him the King's title of Compositeur de la Musique de la Chambre. *Castor and Pollux*, his masterpiece, has recently been revived. When, in 1752, an Italian company brought to Paris a charming opera *La Serva Padrona* of Pergolesi, the city was rent with partisanship, the Coin du Roi, at the opera, supporting Rameau and French classicism, while the Coin de la Reine, consisting largely of admirers of the Frenchman, Lully, was all for Italian entertainment.

In the end, the "old grouch" who with his last breath corrected the priest at his deathbed for intoning off-key, was acknowledged leader of the French school of his day, the contributor of new forms, varied rhythms, rich harmonies and original orchestral effects.

A. Corelli

Arcangelo Corelli
"THE FIRST GREAT FIDDLER"
[Born 1653—Died 1717]

IT IS strange to think that there ever was a day when the violins made by the great Stradivarius, today almost priceless, were unknown and had to be advertised—but such were the times when Arcangelo Corelli lived. He was the first violinist to play a Stradivarius and recommend it to his friends as an instrument worthy of a trial.

When he lived, the art of violin playing was, if not in its infancy, then in its very tender childhood. He raised it to a healthy adolescence. Born in 1653, in Fusignano, a little town in Italy, he early took lessons from Bassani on the violin, and from Simonelli, the Pope's singer, in composition. Stimulated by them to forge ahead and teach himself, he developed a technic of the instrument unequaled in his day.

As the Cardinal Ottoboni, a rich prelate with a passion for music, became his patron, Corelli settled in Rome under his gracious protection. Idolized by king and commoner alike, no lack of appreciation clouded his life. Nor did he suffer from poverty. But he was a simple soul, who clung to suits of sober black while damasks and satins rustled about him, and who walked to the palace, fiddle tucked beneath his arm, rather than pay for a coach. His friend Handel accused him of parsimony but he spent money freely enough on his large collection of paintings and gave generously to charity.

Six impressive tomes contain the twelve *Concerti Grossi* and sixty *Sonatas* which constitute his contribution as composer. The majestic strains of the church music he loved so well echo in the twelve sonatas in Volume I, succeeded by dance-forms—allemande, corrente, giga and others—quaint and tuneful, in Volume II. The noble *La Folia* theme with variations is one of the first solos written for violin alone, yet it has a place in every violinist's repertoire today. Bach, Couperin and Handel were not averse to building upon the foundation laid by the great Italian master.

An untoward incident hastened his death. When quite an old man, he was summoned to play before the King of Naples. As the music was written for a higher position on the violin than he had ever played, he became confused and lapsed into a wrong key. The orchestra stopped while he repeated the passage; he was intensely chagrined and returned to Rome the next day, sunk in melancholy. He died shortly afterward, on January 18, 1717, and was buried with every honor beside his admired Raphael in the Pantheon.

Scarlatti

The Scarlattis

"SERIOUS FATHER, FRIVOLOUS SON"

[Alessandro—Born 1659—Died 1725]
[Domenico—Born 1683—Died 1757]

SERIOUS SCARLATTI," father of Domenico, not only managed to reconcile himself to the frivolities of that wayward genius, his son, but in his operas he reconciled the solemn church chant of Palestrina with the highly expressive and personal note of Monteverdi.

Born in Trapani, Sicily, in 1659, he left his mark on many famous singers, whom he put through their vocal paces at the various conservatories where he taught. His vitality was as high as his originality was low. He produced, with ease, over a hundred operas and two hundred masses, historically distinguished because he relieved the monotony of straight recitativo by introducing the accompaniment and the aria, but of little interest to-day other than historic.

He produced, what is much more important than his writings, a son, Domenico (born in Naples October 12, 1683), who became to the harpsichord what Chopin and Liszt were to the piano. Domenico, taught by his father, started dutifully following in the paternal footsteps, writing operas the very names of which are forgotten today. But as Sir Hubert Parry puts it, he "stepped out with a kind of diabolic masterfulness" on the harpsichord as his true medium.

While Rameau and Couperin were putting forth exquisite bits of French filigree in music, completely characteristic of their period, Scarlatti transfused red blood into Italian harpsichord composition. He wrote short, emphatic pieces of one movement, vigorous, technically complex, melodious, original, and as interesting to audiences to-day as in their own time.

The thrill of crossing hands in playing particularly delighted him until the fat accumulated in a lifetime of eating, drinking, and making merry rendered it impossible for him longer to bring the hands around comfortably. But he solved this problem by writing easier pieces for himself to play.

His meeting with Handel was characteristic. At a masked ball in Venice, Handel was improvising incognito at the harpsichord, when a huge figure in scarlet domino descended upon him, exclaiming, " 'Tis the famous Saxon or the Devil!" The friendship thus initiated survived a contest arranged by Cardinal Ottoboni, wherein Handel carried off the organ prize, but tied with Scarlatti for harpsichord honors.

Domenico died in 1757, leaving a family, a load of gambling debts, and six hundred harpsichord pieces of far greater value, despite his frivolous existence, than the output of his serious father.

G. I. Handel.

Georg Friedrich Handel

"MASTER OF THE ORATORIO"

[Born 1685—Died 1759]

WHEN the *Hallelujah Chorus* from Handel's oratorio *Messiah* pealed forth for the first time, the audience, swayed by an irresistible impulse, rose spontaneously to its feet, as all audiences for two centuries since then have done.

He was one of those natural musicians from whom music gushed like Niagara Falls, a phenomenon the more surprising in that neither his mother, father, nor any discoverable ancestors boasted any trace of such talent.

Georg was born in Halle, Saxony, February 23, 1685, and spent his youth in overcoming paternal opposition to a musical career. At eight, having secretly taught himself to play on a muffled harpsichord smuggled into the attic, he won the privilege of lessons from Zachau, local organist, who taught him four instruments, counterpoint and composition for three years, then confessed the boy knew more than he did.

The study of law, dutifully completed after his father's death in 1697, did not long detain him from his true vocation. As harpsichordist in the Hamburg Theatre, he almost lost his life in a duel with a jealous actor who wanted his job, but a button saved his life in the duel, and his own determination saved the job for him, as it did most things he wanted, until the urge to learn drove him into Italy for three happy, productive years.

England, however, was the scene of his real labors. Two years after his first stay there, in 1710, when his works were wildly acclaimed, he returned for a visit and remained for a lifetime, becoming a naturalized citizen,—grotesque English accent, clumsy German body, and all.

Up to his fiftieth year, he wrote opera endlessly, so shrewdly calculating commercial gain and popular favor that wealth and fame were his for the moment, although only the *Largo* and one or two arias survive on to-day's programs.

It was his failure as opera director in London which drove him to the writing of oratorios. In thirteen years, he produced nineteen,—*Israel in Egypt*, *Herakles*, *The Messiah*, and *Saul* (containing the famous *Dead March*) being the best-known. Innumerable works for flute, violin, organ, harpsichord were tossed off in his spare time. No wonder that he occasionally helped himself to other composers' themes,—he needed them.

No wonder, either, that his health finally failed, and his last years, like Bach's, were spent in blindness and paralysis. "I think I did see all Heaven before me, the great God himself," he said when writing the *Hallelujah Chorus*. Let us hope the vision materialized on that Good Friday, April, 14, 1759, when he breathed his last.

Johann Sebastian Bach

"THE MASTER OF THEM ALL"

[*Born 1685—Died 1750*]

I*N* THE narrow little town of Eisenach, Germany, Johann Sebastian Bach first saw the light, on the 21st of March, 1685. With some two hundred musical ancestors in his family, it was no wonder that the little fellow took to organ, piano, and choir as soon as he could talk. The wonder is that when his elder brother found him copying organ music in the attic at midnight by the light of the moon, he boxed his ears, destroyed the copy, and locked away the original, instead of applauding the little boy's industry.

But he grew up, for all that, and raised on his own account, with the help of two successive wives, a jolly family of twenty children, to whom he was as kindly as his elders had been severe with him. Many were the happy evenings he spent in his big armchair, with his mug of ale, his pipe, and perhaps a child or two on his lap, listening to children and friends singing his chorales, or playing his latest motet, or fugue, or piece for violin, flute, cello, or clavichord. Sometimes he would rise and improvise a new piece for them.

Despite the difficulty of feeding such a family, he was always serene in their midst. He had, too, the serenity that springs from a deeply religious nature. First he was choir-boy at Lüneburg, then organist in the church at Arnstadt, then for many years, concert-master to the Duke of Weimar, then court director at Köthen, and again, at the end of his life, organist at Leipsic. But wherever his lot was cast, he dedicated all the music he unceasingly produced to the God he worshipped and served.

The list of his music is endless. His vocal works include five complete sets of cantatas; five *Passions*, among them the famous Easter *Passion According to St. Matthew;* the giant *B Minor Mass*, and many others. Among his instrumental works we think at once of the *Three Part Inventions*, the *Piano Suites*, the *Forty-Eight Preludes and Fugues*, the *Well-Tempered Clavichord*, and countless organ and other compositions.

His unremitting industry resulted in the loss of his eyesight, and for three years before his death on July 28, 1750, he had to dictate all his compositions. Yet he never complained, but died, as he had lived, praising God from his death-bed in one of the most beautiful of chorales.

Joseph Haydn

Franz Joseph Haydn

"PAPA HAYDN"

[Born 1732—Died 1809]

ONE of a dozen brothers and sisters, born March 31, 1732, of a humble wheelwright and a cook, in Rohrau, Austria, Franz Joseph Haydn was eminently a child of the people. The school of hard knocks was his preparation for a life of incredible industry.

A cousin, Frankh, took him from home at the age of six to train his voice, but woefully neglected to feed and clothe him at the same time, and when he was sent to the choir-school in Vienna the fulness of his working day there was balanced by the emptiness of his stomach. Yet he scraped together enough pence to buy two second-hand books on harmony, since nobody undertook to teach him any, and when he was put out of the choir-school for cutting off the pigtail of the man in front of him, his two precious books went with him to the attic refuge offered him by his friend, Spangler.

A score composed for the actor, Kurz; a job accompanying, bootblacking and valeting Porpora, the singer; tireless teaching and composing held at bay the wolf ever growling at his door until, miraculously, his daily bread was assured by wealthy patrons.

His thirty years with the Esterhazys, his choicest patrons, were ideal. Summers he passed on their princely country estate, winters in Vienna, with festivals galore for which he composed and conducted one lovely program after another. Over a hundred symphonies, forty of his eighty-five string quartettes, a vast number of concerti, and an oratorio mark these serene years.

Hospitable England welcomed him so warmly in 1791 that he remarked "It is England that has made me famous in Germany." *The Creation* and *The Seasons* were his oratorio tribute to his English friends and his *Surprise Symphony* a humorous dig at their napping proclivities.

We cannot list his 1047 works, so full of charm and beauty. Many of the shorter pieces are prolonged laughs, bubbling with happy melody and humor. He added the murmur of muted strings and the clear song of the clarinet to the voices of the orchestra which he further enriched by writing parts in such fashion as to bring out the individual tone-color of each voice. The elementary sonata-form he developed, adding a second theme to relieve the monotony of but one. Teacher of Beethoven and Mozart, "Papa Haydn" to a musical generation, he could truly boast that "My language is understood by the whole world."

Luigi Boccherini

Luigi Boccherini

NICKNAMED "THE WIFE OF HAYDN"

[Born 1743—Died 1805]

A PERPETUAL fountain of music, with a stop-cock to be turned on or off as desired,—that is the description given of Luigi Boccherini. Called the "wife of Haydn" because his chamber music so closely resembled that contemporary's, he has his own particular claim to fame, nevertheless, for he brought the cello part (the cello being his own instrument) into a prominent place in the string quartette, where Haydn had always relegated it to the humble task of accompanying the first violin.

As he wrote under patronage, with the assurance of immediate performance, his output was enormous. He was born in Lucca, Italy, February 19, 1743, and his father, a contrabass player, was his first teacher, but a teacher with sufficient wisdom to pack the boy off to Rome, to study violin, cello, and composition with Abbé Vanucci, as soon as he recognized his unusual talent. Luigi's friendship with the violinist Manfredi in Rome ripened into an artistic partnership, and together they started concertizing, arriving finally at the court of Charles IV, in Madrid.

Here they received such a warm Spanish welcome that they remained. Boccherini, with a fat annuity and the added honor of being court favorite, found himself with nothing to do in return except to turn out trios, quartettes, quintettes, violin or cello pieces, and occasional symphonies or operas, which he did with consummate ease.

All went well until the fatal day when the King objected to a certain passage in a new trio as being hackneyed. Boccherini agreed to correct it, but impudently doubled its repetition instead. Whereupon the King, infuriated at the implied slur on his musicality, forthwith dismissed him in disgrace.

Another patron was found, the French consul Lucien Buonaparte, for whose musicales Boccherini's fountain of inspiration played merrily. But Buonaparte was recalled, and Luigi fell upon evil days. The story of his last years is a sad record of illness and poverty. He was reduced to making guitar arrangements for wealthy amateurs, and selling his compositions for practically nothing at all. His death on May 28, 1805, was a release from misery.

In his voluminous output,—125 string quintettes, 91 string quartettes, 54 string trios, 20 symphonies, and cello and violin pieces,—flowing, original melody, and harpsichordian delicacy and refinement are always present. No wonder the court ladies pointed their little toes with such stately zest to the strains of the famous *Boccherini Minuet*, which wafts to us today the perfume of their dainty presence.

da L. Cherubini

Luigi Maria Cherubini

"THE ITALIAN WHO COMPOSED GERMAN MUSIC IN FRANCE"

[Born 1760—Died 1842]

A LONG name, a long and honorable career of teaching and composing, a long catalog of compositions, and oblivion for most of them,—that, in a word, is the story of Cherubini. But *he* is remembered, if his works are not, because of his profound influence upon music, because he injected into French opera the dramatic quality of the German and influenced succeeding composers to do likewise, because he was the first to make use of the English horn and solo cello in the orchestra, and because he clarified many rules of counterpoint in his masterly treatise on the subject.

He was born in Florence September 14, 1760. A student by nature, he applied himself at an early age to absorbing all the musical teachings he could lay hands on. His father, who was a theatre harpsichordist, as well as numerous teachers of composition, subjected him to a rigorous drill, the theory being that the drier learning was, the more thorough it must be. Finding a wretched fiddle at home, he taught himself to play so acceptably that on one occasion, when he was about ten, he slipped in and substituted, unobserved, for an absent violinist in the theatre orchestra. Eventually he became, according to some estimates, the most accomplished musician of the nineteenth century.

During his first period, 1760–1791, he wrote chiefly sacred music and light opera in the Italian style; the second period, 1791–1813, was devoted to the composition of his greatest operas,—*Medée, Faniska, Abencerrages, Lodoiska,* and *Les Deux Journées (The Water Carrier).* On the strength of the two last, Beethoven dubbed him the greatest composer of his time.

As despotic Director of the Conservatoire in Paris from 1821–1841, he was more feared than loved, even by his wife and three children. When Liszt and Rubinstein applied for admission, he actually rejected them, and he made Berlioz' student life thoroughly miserable by frowning upon his musical ideas as too radical. Dignified conservatism was his platform. The fiery eyes under beetling brows atop the small body darted their lightnings as balefully upon Napoleon, when he availed himself of his imperial privilege of meddling in the affairs of the Conservatoire, as upon the humblest student.

A picturesque figure, this "Italian who composed German music in France," music replete with color and melody, a model of classic form. When death took him, on May 15, 1842, from his meticulously neat little office, it removed the greatest teaching and organizing force of his century.

Mozart

Wolfgang Amadeus Mozart

"SUPER-MAN AND SUPER-MUSICIAN"

[Born 1756—Died 1791]

A LITTLE boy in white peruke and satin knee-breeches whose feet barely reached the pedals, but whose hands performed astounding feats of dexterity on the keyboard, left the town of Salzburg, in Austria, where he was born January 27, 1756, to play his way into the hearts of all who heard him, from the crusty customs official who tried to detain him at the border to Princess Marie Antoinette in her royal nursery. That little boy was Mozart and the love his childish performance aroused grew as the boy became man, virtuoso and composer.

He appears to have come into the world bursting with melodies which his father's strict musical training, added to his own genius, released with a spontaneity that is a never-ending source of wonder. An incessant inner life of creation went on wherever he happened to be, and the whistling, humming or tapping which were its outward manifestations gave only the faintest indication of its intensity. Every piece of music he wrote (six hundred in his thirty-six years) was complete in his mind before a note was transferred to paper.

The life of such a genius should have been successful and prosperous, but it was neither. After his early triumphs he took service with the Archbishop of Salzburg, a churlish patron whose exactions would have dried up a stream of inspiration less sparkling than Mozart's. Unrequited affection for a singer further depressed him. The popularity of his music enriched only the publisher, never the composer.

In 1781 he settled in Vienna, marrying Constance von Weber, sister of his first love. She waltzed with him to keep warm when there was no money for coal; she cut his meat lest he injure his precious hands; she condoned his extravagances; she welcomed his friends, Haydn among them, and rejoiced when he and the latter each paid graceful tribute to the chamber-music of the other. His gay operas, *The Marriage of Figaro*, *Cosi Fan Tutti*, *The Magic Flute*, and *Don Juan* were written during these lean years, as were about twenty-five piano concertos, seven for violin, forty-nine symphonies, innumerable church, instrumental, orchestral, and chamber-works, all masterpieces of absolute beauty.

An unfortunate commission to write a requiem mass for an anonymous patron so depressed him that he was convinced it was for his own funeral. On the day of its completion he sank into profound melancholy and died that same night, December 5, 1791. A pauper's grave was the last resting-place of this great genius of the classical period.

Ludwig Van Beethoven

"THE COLOSSUS OF MUSIC"

[*Born 1770—Died 1827*]

THIS giant came of a pigmy race. His father was a drunken band-musician, his mother a cook. He was born in Bonn, Germany, December 17, 1770, and here he spent a poverty-ridden and unhappy youth, beaten by his father when he failed to practice the piano, but making a creditable public appearance as a pianist at the age of eight.

A few encouraging words from Mozart, whom he met in Vienna when he was sixteen, gave him a ray of hope, but months of weary drudgery teaching in Bonn almost extinguished it, until, in desperation, he returned to Vienna, resolved to study with Haydn and support himself as best he could.

For the next few years in Vienna he flourished exceedingly. He and his compositions and his piano playing were everywhere welcomed. Friends appeared on all sides. Great ladies went on their knees to beg him to play for them, and he refused or consented, as his mood of the moment dictated. He called his friend and patron, Prince Lichnowsky, a donkey, and the prince smiled and continued to be his friend.

But this period of happy productivity was of all too short duration. In 1800 he noticed with horror that he was becoming deaf. Panic seized him. He left Vienna and shut himself up in the country. But he continued composing, and in the music of this period we find poured forth the expression of his intense personal emotions. The years 1800–1816, known as his Middle Period, mark the transition from the classic to the romantic composers who came later.

Unfortunately, his disposition declined with his hearing. He became morose, suspicious, quarrelsome. But the music of his last period, from 1816 to his death, March 26, 1827, is the greatest of all. He could not hear the applause that greeted his *Ninth Symphony* when he conducted it, but he could hear in his mind the melodies he had to write; thus his later music is more intellectual, losing, however, none of the expressive quality of his Middle Period.

Nine symphonies, among them the beloved *Fifth*, an opera, *Fidelio*, a quantity of chamber music, and instrumental compositions such as the famous *Moonlight Sonata* and *Violin Concerto* attest his greatness. It is sad to record that this Genius of Geniuses died in poverty, of pneumonia contracted while driving home in an open cart from the country home of a brother so parsimonious that he denied him the closed carriage which might have saved his life.

Franz Peter Schubert

"THE LARK AT HEAVEN'S GATE SINGING"

[Born 1797—Died 1828]

THE thirty-one years of Schubert's life are a "Moment Musical" in eternity, but a moment so musical that never-to-be-forgotten strains of melody survive its passing and vitalize his fame as the first truly romantic composer.

A flabby, be-spectacled little man with shy, stammering speech and self-effacing personality, yet with a magnetic quality that attracted many friends—such was Franz Schubert. As his mother, a cook, and his father, a schoolmaster, produced thirteen children besides Franz in the village near Vienna where he was born in 1797, there was neither time nor money for adoring concentration upon his precocious musical talents.

The Konviktschule, in Vienna, to which his fresh soprano voice gained him admittance, when Salieri was on the point of denying it to so uncouth and ill-clad an applicant, gave him his education. While enjoying semi-starvation on two scanty meals daily, he conducted and played in the orchestra, sang in the choir and studied the usual school subjects. Too poor to buy music-paper, he found a friend, Spaun, who provided him with it, whereupon the hungry fifteen-year-old produced two string-quartettes, a trio, an orchestral overture and sundry pieces, despite Salieri's indifference to teaching him harmony and counterpoint.

During his next few years, in his father's school, the music in his soul spilled so freely on his pupil's exercise books, in lieu of corrections, that at last he was permitted to withdraw. And withdraw he did, to a cold, dingy, little room where he sat all day in a dressing-gown composing, issuing forth only in the evenings for convivial café sessions with his friends. For a while young von Schober gave him a home; then the poet Mayrhofer, many of whose poems he set to music; then Count Esterhazy.

All this time his compositions brought him no money; many were rescued from oblivion years later by Schumann, who found them on a dusty shelf and carried them to Mendelssohn to give to the world. The opera *Rosamunde*, nine symphonies, much chamber music and a wealth of lovely songs, including "*Hark, hark the Lark*" and "*Who is Sylvia?*" remain. Extreme sweetness, warm lyrical beauty, intensely personal emotional expression—all these characteristics of the romantic school are his.

Beethoven's appreciation won him Schubert's adoring, if inarticulate, friendship. It was only a few months after the latter had been a weeping torchbearer at the Master's funeral that he himself succumbed to typhoid fever, and was laid to rest near his great friend and inspiration in Vienna.

Johann Strauss

Johann Strauss

(FATHER AND SON) "THE WALTZ KINGS"

[Father—Born 1804—Died 1849]
[Son—Born 1825—Died 1899]

WHAT the Wrights are to aeroplanes, the Strausses are to the waltz. It is difficult to conceive of a world empty of waltzes, but so it was before Johann Strauss, the elder, came into it with the 19th century. Three-quarter time there had been, but real waltz music, languishing, swirling, enticing, in which the very soul might be lost in an ecstacy of motion—this it remained, strangely enough, for the Victorian era to develop.

The elder Strauss, whom Wagner dubbed "the demon of the folk-spirit," like the Pied Piper of Hamlin, enticed his fellow-Austrians up the Danube to follow him about from tavern to tavern, from city to city, to dance to his fiddling. Later, his wanderings took him all over Europe, where his success was crowned simultaneously with the coronation of Victoria.

Sensing that his sons, Johann, Joseph and Edouard, might outstrip his fame, he tried to divert them into banking and similar unmusical pursuits, but they had inherited too much of his own "genius for joy." The battle of Strauss vs. Strauss—of father against sons, for the title of Waltz King—rent the musical world for many years. Beginning when the first-born and namesake placarded Vienna with notices that he would conduct an orchestra to play his father's compositions and his own and the world could then decide who was the greater, it ended in a reconciliation only a few years before the elder's death. Whatever may have been the opinion of their contemporaries, Time pronounced its own verdict, for the compositions which come to mind immediately when the name of Strauss is mentioned— "*The Blue Danube,*" "*Wienerblut,*" "*Kuenstlerleben,*" "*Die Fledermaus*" and "*Eine Nacht in Venedig*"—were all the products of the *younger* Johann.

Four hundred waltzes, countless light operas, engagements to conduct in all the capitals of Europe and an orchestra of his own in Vienna, made his a full and rich existence. On Independence Day in 1872, he conducted a monster chorus of 1000 voices with 100 assistant conductors at Gilmore's International Peace Jubilee in Boston. Although he was paid lavishly for this one appearance and was offered every inducement to tour the country, he considered this tour de force sufficient for the United States and returned to a less demanding Europe to live his three-score-ten and more, a jubilant, gay spirit to the end.

Felix Mendelssohn Bartholdy

Felix Mendelssohn-Bartholdy

"DARLING OF THE GODS"

[Born 1809—Died 1847]

*I*T IS meet that the fairy-music in the scherzo of Mendelssohn's *Midsummer Night's Dream Overture* should be of his loveliest, if it glorifies the good fairies who undoubtedly hovered over the cradle in Hamburg in which he found himself on February 3, 1809. Not alone fairies, but loving, intelligent parents and the best of tutors supervised the education of this favored princeling who enjoyed all the material satisfactions supplied by wealth, all the spiritual peace engendered by love.

As a handsome little boy, he might have been found almost any Sunday morning in the music room of the Mendelssohn home, assembling his orchestra of brother, sisters, and friends and wielding the baton while they played the pieces he composed for them. All Hamburg flocked to these musicales, and by the time Felix was sixteen and launching on his first tour he was already known as a pianist, organist, viola player, conductor and composer. His triumphs abroad, where such men as Goethe, Liszt, Chopin, Schumann, Rossini, Meyerbeer vied for his friendship, so established him that he eventually became a powerful influence upon the musical life of his generation.

A performance of the *St. Matthew Passion* of Bach, which he conducted when but nineteen, opened his eyes to the wealth of Bach music which had lain neglected for half a century. It opened the eyes of others as well, and paved the way for the formation of the Bach Gesellschaft in 1850, which later issued a complete edition of the Master's works. Had he done nothing else, this service would insure his fame, but he did much on his own account besides. He founded the first German Conservatory of Music in Leipsic. He conducted and taught all over the map of Europe. *The Midsummer Night's Dream Overture*, written at seventeen; the flowing violin concerto which has borne many a virtuoso to fame on its limpid rhythms; the *Fingal's Cave Overture, Scottish* and *Italian Symphonies* and much chamber music reveal him as a romantic steeped in classic tradition, an expressionistic conservative. They are the sincere, often inspired reflections of the personality of a completely charming and cultured gentleman.

A happy marriage, every musical honor, the sympathetic companionship of his sister Fanny, hardly less gifted than he, filled his cup to overflowing. However, when he was thirty-eight, Fanny's death shocked him out of his paradise. Coming when he was over-tired and run-down, it proved too great a shock for the sensitive nature inured only to happiness. A few months later (November 4, 1847) he, too, was laid to rest.

Robert Schumann
Clara Schumann

Klara and Robert Schumann

"THE BROWNINGS OF MUSIC"

[Klara—Born 1819—Died 1896]
[Robert—Born 1810—Died 1856]

THE fourfold struggle that was Robert Schumann's life began with his birth in Saxony, June 10, 1810. When he was graduated from the University of Leipsic, supposedly a lawyer, he wrote his mother, pathetically: "My whole life has been a twenty-years' battle between poesy and prose—or call it music and law." With music triumphant, this first phase of the conflict of inclination and filial duty came to an end and almost immediately he entered upon the second.

Papa Wieck, his piano teacher, had a daughter, Klara, whose piano performances at nine were the talk of Leipsic. She adored Robert, fed him gingerbread and played his pieces entrancingly. Her image persisted in Robert's otherwise fickle fancy, and when he saw her again, at eighteen, he proceeded to woo her in passionate piano pieces, despite Wieck's opposition to their meeting "on pain of death." Finally, after difficulties culminating in a lawsuit, he won his mate and his second battle.

His joy in her congenial companionship and magnificent piano-playing resulted in a great burst of composition. Over one hundred surpassing songs, with accompaniments as individual as the voice parts, three great symphonies, many string quartettes and the famous piano quintette were born in the five happy years following his marriage. The *Kreisleriana*, *Carnaval* and *Davidsbündlertänze* the *Kinderscenen*, *Papillons* and many other piano pieces rippled from his soul and from Klara's magic fingers in characteristic Schumann terms of brilliant and extravagant effects, humor and lovely melody combined with deep poetic feeling.

With pen in hand he conducted the third phase of conflict for truth and sincerity in music against the Philistinism of cheap facility. All of the romantic composers, including Chopin, Mendelssohn, and Brahms, owe an undying debt of gratitude to the encouraging support of his critical articles in *Die Neue Zeitschrift für Musik*. But the fourth and bitterest battle was a losing one, despite Klara's unremitting care. Even in his university days, he had suffered from fits of black depression. As his labors of writing, teaching, conducting and composing became more taxing, the attacks became more frequent, complicated by delusions and noises in the head. Finally he sought escape from "mortal anguish of mind" by throwing himself from a high bridge into the Rhine. Rescued by a passing fishing-boat, he took refuge in an asylum where he died (July 29, 1856) in his Klara's arms. She survived him by forty years of loving dedication to the perpetuation of his fame.

Franz Liszt

Franz Liszt

"THE FEARLESS CHAMPION OF THE NEW"

[Born 1811—Died 1886]

A LONG-HAIRED, long-fingered gypsy pianist in his youth, a benign white-haired abbé in later life, but in each aspect possessing all the charm of the other,—such was Franz Liszt.

He was born in Raiding, Hungary, on October 22, 1811, and evinced such talent at an early age that several nobles undertook to finance his musical education. He worked with the best teachers, Czerny and Salieri, besides his devoted father, and appeared before an enthusiastic public in Vienna at the age of eleven, when Beethoven set the seal of approval on his performance.

In France he was hailed as "Lits, la Neuvième Merveille du Monde." It was in France where he heard the wizard violinist Paganini, was fired with a desire to emulate at the piano his diabolical technical brilliance, and succeeded. In France, also, he met Chopin, and Berlioz, and Mme. La Comtesse d'Agoult, his intimate friend and mother of his three children.

From 1833 to 1848, he enjoyed a series of phenomenal artistic successes in all parts of the world. His personal charm plus his genius carried all before them. The wealth which flowed in he dispensed with gypsy generosity, not only in the name of charity, but in so graceful a gesture as paying for the completion of the Beethoven statue at Bonn when work was discontinued due to lack of funds.

When he retired from the concert stage in 1848, he devoted himself to teaching, conducting, writing, and composing. He had some three hundred private pupils, among them the most illustrious pianists of the present day. He conducted the opera at Weimar, seizing every opportunity to offer new works. His motto was "First place to the living," and in pursuance thereof he produced Wagner's *Lohengrin*, *Flying Dutchman*, and *Tannhäuser*, Berlioz' *Benvenuto Cellini*, Weber's *Euryanthe*, Schumann's *Manfred*, and many others.

Rome and Catholicism claimed him in 1861. He donned the abbé's long black robe, and his music also took on priestly vestments. Instead of fiery Hungarian rhapsodies or orchestral transcriptions for the piano, a requiem or an oratorio flowed from his peaceful pen. But he continued to teach and conduct in Weimar and Budapest, while living in Rome as the Pope's Palestrina.

He died, appropriately enough, at the Wagner festival in Baireuth, on July 13, 1886, while visiting his daughter, Cosima. Dazzling virtuoso, conductor and composer, teacher, apostle of new music, champion of romanticism, writer and editor, friend of rich and poor, he had many claims to fame.

Ant Rubinstein.

Anton Gregor Rubinstein

"RUSSIA'S WANDERING MINSTREL"

[Born 1829—Died 1894]

WHEN Anton, son of the pencil-maker Rubinstein of Wechwotinez, was but a year old, the Czar issued such a severe ukase against the Jews that his family decided that, in order to survive, they must renounce their faith. Accordingly, little Anton was baptized, but the warm emotional quality of the Jew persisted in him and in his music, despite all the cold holy water sprinkled upon him.

When the Rubinstein covered wagon came creaking into Moscow, Anton was a bright little boy of five. He had had a few piano lessons from his mother, and immediately started working with Villoing, then the best piano teacher in Moscow. He displayed such remarkable talent that his wise mother never sent him to school, but had him tutored at home. His appearance as an infant prodigy at the age of ten justified this course of action, and covered him with glory, as did his subsequent concert tour.

There came bad months, however, after his father's death. When he was sixteen, he was left to support himself in Berlin, where he was studying harmony, while his mother and brother returned to Russia. After two years, he decided that his future lay in his own native land, but he had great difficulty in getting back into it. Having left Russia as a child, he had no passport, and had to play the piano for an unconvinced official to prove that he was, as represented, a pianist. Moreover, his trunk full of music manuscript was confiscated on suspicion of harboring Nihilist propaganda and two years' work was lost, the manuscript being later sold by the pound as waste paper.

But once in Russia, he found friends and recognition everywhere, and at the age of twenty-three was accounted an artist of high standing. He made many tours to all parts of the world, always returning between trips to the wife and children who created a happy home-life for him in his beloved St. Petersburg. The St. Petersburg Conservatory, founded in 1862 as a result of his urging, gave him another foothold there, for he became its director, and devoted much time to teaching there and much money to its financial support.

On his American tour, in 1872, he played two hundred and fifteen concerts in which his own compositions, among them the "*Kamennoi Ostrow*" for the piano, and his innumerable songs, such as "*Melody in F*," were hailed with enthusiasm, despite his compatriots' criticism of their German tendencies. He died in Russia November 20, 1894, aged sixty-five.

Hector Berlioz

Hector Berlioz

"A PROPHET WITHOUT HONOR IN HIS OWN COUNTRY"

[Born 1803—Died 1869]

For most people, it is a far cry from the dissecting room to the Conservatory, but for ardent, determined young Hector Berlioz, as fiery in his nature as in his hair, it was but a step.

Son of a country physician in Côte-St.-André, near Lyons, France, where he was born December 11, 1803, he grew up hedged about with the comforts, as well as restrictions, of the small-town bourgeois. His escape from tamely inheriting his father's practice, to becoming a musician, was dramatically achieved against dire parental opposition. In Côte-St.-André, nice people did not become musicians.

His career in the Conservatoire was stormy, for Cherubini, its head, strongly disapproved of the young radical and his original ideas, and withheld the Prix de Rome from him for three successive years, in the course of which he almost starved as a chorus man in a Parisian theatre.

Having finally gained the Prix, he crowned his student career with a concert, where his prize *Cantata* and *Symphonie Fantastique* were applauded by Liszt. In 1834, when he conducted his *Harold Symphony* in Paris after his return from Rome, Paganini rushed to the platform, covered Berlioz' hand with kisses, commissioned him to write him a viola concerto, and gave him twenty thousand francs.

This was a bright moment, but there were many dark ones. He married Henrietta Smithson, an English actress, whom he wooed, to her bewilderment, as dramatically as he did everything else. But this marriage ended tragically in a divorce, and his second marriage, years later, also proved unsuccessful.

His great symphonic poems *Romeo et Juliette* and *Benvenuto Cellini*, and the dramatic legend *La Damnation de Faust* were received with such apathy by his Parisian audiences that, after each failure, he was impelled to escape from Paris and tour in Russia, England, Germany and Austria. Everywhere excepting in Paris his works were received with enthusiasm. Finally, election to the Académie, and the Légion d'Honneur, could no longer be denied him. He even became Librarian at the Conservatoire, though the post of harmony professor was refused him because he could not play the piano. A master of orchestral idiom, his music was stormy, like himself, his conceptions immense and original.

The failure of his last opera, *Les Troyens*, which was hissed off the Paris stage, the death of his son Louis, and his own nervous malady caused the final breakdown, and in March, 1869, he crept to the south of France to die.

Frédéric François Chopin

"THE SUPREME POET OF THE PIANO"

[Born 1809—Died 1849]

HATS off, gentlemen, a genius!" wrote Schumann about the young Chopin.

Delicate, fastidious, sensitive, content with nothing short of perfection, and perpetually suffering because so few things are perfect, Frédéric Chopin endured his existence in an imperfect world as genius must, and of his suffering was born some of the finest piano music ever written.

Born near Warsaw, in the town of Zelasowa-Wola, March 1, 1809, of a French father and a Polish mother, he was gently reared in an atmosphere of sunshine, flowers and charming friendships, with three adoring sisters to play make-believe with him.

His first teacher of composition said, "Let him alone. He treads an extraordinary path because he has extraordinary gifts, and follows no method, but creates one." Truly he invented no new forms, but within the limitations of the old ones—the waltz, the prelude, the nocturne, the polonaise, the scherzo, the sonata,—he wrote music for the piano, evoking effects of delicacy, romance, poetry, and strength which had never been known before.

Although passionately a Polish patriot, he lived most of his life in Paris where his triumphs at the age of twenty-one were phenomenal. Modestly he wrote to his family, "I move in the highest circles and I don't know how I got there!" Delacroix, Liszt, Heine, Schumann, Mendelssohn were his friends; and were proud to be invited to those intimate evenings which he so infinitely preferred to concert appearances, when he sat at the piano in his fire-lit drawing room and played, as only he could play, for three or four rapt listeners.

Many friends he met through George Sand, that masculine figure of a woman who took the sensitive, ailing being under her large wing and repeatedly nursed him back to health when his lungs began to fail him. He swore to die in her arms only, but there was a quarrel, their beautiful friendship was broken, and not only did he not die in her arms but he actually refused to see her when she came to call during his last illness.

Like Paderewski, he put love of country above all else, and poured out much of it in the stirring *Polonaises*, the *Krakowiak in F*, and *Fantaisie on Polish Airs*. When he died, October 17, 1849, his coffin was gently sprinkled with Polish earth in recognition of this love, and he was laid to rest among the great musicians of the land of his adoption.

Cesar Granck

César Franck

"PATER SERAPHICUS"

[*Born 1822—Died 1890*]

*I*N THE dingy organ-loft at St. Clothilde, removed from the world's vanities by a steep narrow stairway, César Franck was wont to sit for hours before his organ. As marvelous improvisations melted from his fingers, those with him saw him surrounded, as it were, with an aureole, while his listeners felt that the spirit of Bach had returned to earth.

But the organ-loft was inaccessible. He was modest and retiring, concentrated upon art, not fame—a teaching saint. So this gentle soul, the greatest French genius of his century, known as "that little man who teaches at the Conservatoire, whose trousers are too short," was denied even the satisfaction of being director of his department until he had taught harmony there for some years; saw Gounod depart, noisily disapproving, from a performance of his great oratorio *Redemption;* and was condemned to live laboriously in obscurity. But there was no resentment in his soul.

César was born in Liège, Belgium, December 10, 1822, and attended the Conservatory there and later the Conservatoire in Paris. When, in 1848, he married the young actress of his choice, the wedding party had to climb over barricaded streets to enter the church. Even as Paris was in a state of revolution, so was Franck who, by this bold stroke, deposed the paternal tyrant who had expected to live from the exploitation of his son's talent.

Years of hard work followed, teaching for ten hours a day, fulfilling his duties as organist of St. Clothilde and at the Conservatoire. But a few hours daily were religiously reserved for composition. The oratorio, *Ruth*, some trios and piano pieces constituted his early works, while his middle period witnessed the production of glorious masses and organ pieces, with *Redemption* as the high point. Orchestral works, including the great *D Minor Symphony*, two operas, the violin sonata, string quartette and the mystic *Beatitudes*, which contain all the philosophy of his meditative later years, conclude the list of his important works.

Pleurisy, aggravated by a neglected injury received when an omnibus struck him, caused his death on November 8, 1890. His pupils, d'Indy, Chausson, Chabrier, Fauré, paid him loving tribute and his naïve remark after the performance of his quartette, "Voilà le public qui commence a me comprendre" has been realized at last.

Saint-Saëns

Camille Saint-Saëns
"THE COMPLETE FRENCHMAN"
[Born 1835—Died 1921]

*I*N HIS memoirs, Saint-Saëns relates how, as a child of two, he took keen musical delight in such homely sounds as the crescendo of the singing tea-kettle, the creaking of a door, or a chiming clock. So it did not surprise his mother, an artist, that, thanks to the intelligent teaching of a great-aunt, he became a child prodigy who gave his first public piano recital at six and a half and continued to give concerts until he was over eighty years old. When she was criticized for allowing his baby fingers to attempt a Beethoven sonata and was asked, "What music will he play when he is twenty?" she replied with calm certainty, "He will play his own."

Her prophecy was verified. The delicate baby born in Paris on October 9, 1835, lived to become not only a brilliant virtuoso pianist but a composer of tremendous versatility and an influential critic. He failed of the Prix de Rome when graduated from the Conservatoire, Berlioz (who later called him "one of the greatest composers of our epoch") voting against him with the statement, "He knows everything, but he lacks experience."

Despite that single failure, his education was completely rounded, and he illustrated nobly his own contention that "the understanding for and appreciation of beautiful harmonic successions is only possible to a public moving on a pinnacle of culture." Symphonies and symphonic poems, chamber-music, songs, concertos, oratorios, operas, transcriptions bore witness to the complex abilities of this composer whose works were both classical and romantic and who also wrote program music. His symphonic poems, *Le Rouet d' Omphale*, *Phaeton*, *Danse Macabre* and *La Jeunesse d'Hercule* became at once extremely popular. One of the first Frenchmen to grasp the thunderous meanings of Wagner, he won that gentleman's difficult praise for his opera *Samson et Delilah*, wherein he practiced the Wagnerian principles of powerful themes and rich orchestration.

Taxed by the critics of his own day, in the same breath, with lack of originality and with too daring innovations, he is to-day considered somewhat old-fashioned, "a paler repetition of a pale Mendelssohn." In personal charm, conversational ability, in the breadth of his travels and reading, in the influence he exerted through the *Société Nationale de Musique* on the musical thought of his generation, in a certain happy facility of invention, he did indeed resemble Mendelssohn. Yet he was the complete Frenchman who left, when he died in Algiers on December 16, 1921, a huge musical legacy as completely French as himself.

Bedř. Smetana

Frederick Smetana
"WHO GAVE LUSTRE TO THE NAME OF BOHEMIA"
[Born 1824—Died 1884]

ALTHOUGH his life was darkened by the loss of wife and daughter, his hearing and his sanity hopelessly impaired during his last years, this Bohemian composer gave birth to music that is infectiously gay, lilting and spirited, and of so marked a national character that he is known as the founder of the school of modern Czech music, even as Grieg is of the Norwegian.

Born March 2, 1824, in Litomysl, practically self-taught until his twentieth year, he was sufficiently a prodigy to play first violin in a Haydn quartette at five. During his school years, he formed his own quartette, whose members being too poor to buy music, used to send Frederick to the band-concerts where for one groschen he could drink in the harmonies of Beethoven and the other great masters, then hasten home to set them down on paper for his group to perform. At this time he noted modestly in his diary: "I wish to become a Mozart in composition and a Liszt in technique."

His father, however, had other ambitions—he was to be a lawyer. Much discussion ensued before he was permitted to go to Prague to study music and starve. Free piano lessons through the intercession of his fiancée, Katerina Kolar, a position as resident music-master with Count Thun, and the opening of a private music school ended this period of his career. Liszt, that admirable publicity agent, had become his friend; other distinguished musicians followed suit.

After a stay in Gothenburg, he returned to Prague in 1858, to take up the cudgels in behalf of Bohemian music, until then almost an unknown quantity. He organized subscription concerts, which became the Czech Philharmonic Society, an experimental National Theater, a Society of Bohemian Artists. His own compositions flowed in a sparkling stream. He wrote eight patriotic operas, among them the popular *Bartered Bride* and *The Kiss*, six symphonic poems, ranking with the operas in pictorial nationalism, the epic string quartette (E Minor) *Aus Meinem Leben*, a trio and numerous bright piano pieces, featuring the Czech polka much as Chopin did the Polish mazurka.

But now the noises in his head, which had afflicted him increasingly since his becoming totally deaf in 1881, drowned out all else. Too distracted to attend the concert in honor of his sixtieth birthday in March, 1884, he withdrew to an asylum, where on May 12 the joy-giver died in gloom. With Dvořák he gave lustre to the name of Bohemia in the realm of music.

Antonín Dvořák

Antonin Dvořák

"HE MADE SYMPHONIES OUT OF FOLK SONGS"

[Born 1841—Died 1904]

A BOHEMIAN peasant, with all the peasant's love of color, of stamping rhythms and bright melody, Antonin Dvořák was, after Smetana, the first creator of a national Bohemian music.

Son of the jolly innkeeper in the sleepy village of Mühlhausen, the swarthy, black-eyed lad passed a happy youth with village tunes and village dances all about him.

A year as innkeeper-butcher at fifteen convinced him that sausage-making was not his vocation, and he persuaded his father, against strong opposition, to allow him to enter the Orgelschule at Prague. Handicapped by lack of money, without books or scores or music-paper, with only what he could earn playing at cafés or through an occasional engagement at the opera under Smetana, he still managed to be graduated in 1860 and win the second prize. And he managed to spend the next twelve years studying, in his poor lodgings, from borrowed scores, the works of the great masters. If ever a knight earned his spurs by fasting and prayer, he was that knight.

The first composition to which he applied his study, an opera *King and Collier* reeked of German influence and failed dismally. But he retrieved himself by writing a stirring national song, which caught his countrymen like wildfire. The *Slavonic Dances*, produced in 1878, brought him fame overnight, thanks partly to Liszt, their publicity agent in Germany. Dvořák went to bed one night comparatively unknown, and awoke to find himself hailed in Germany and England as a great Bohemian composer.

Americans love him especially because, while he was director of the New York Conservatory from 1892–95, he became so much interested in the negro tunes sung for him by one of his students, that he embodied them in the *New World Symphony*. It took a Bohemian to recognize that America had a folk-music!

He should have been happy in America, where he was appreciated, but homesickness drove him back to Prague to spend the last years of his life composing, and directing the Conservatory there. He died May 1, 1904.

The wild rhythms of the Czech "furiant" and the melancholy lilt of the "dumka," masterly orchestration, naturalness and sincerity of expression give romantic warmth and color to the five symphonies, symphonic poems, chamber music, violin *Humoreske*, and songs, which make them popular in the best sense,—beloved by the people.

Stephen C. Foster

Stephen Foster

"CREATOR OF AMERICAN FOLK-MUSIC"

[Born 1826—Died 1864]

AN INDIVIDUAL who wrote songs for a whole people; who created music expressing the soul of a folk he did not know; scion of a family of ardent anti-abolitionists, he became the spokesman for the misunderstood negro; a musical best-seller whose compositions, translated and sung in every tongue, brought him no affluence—this contradiction in terms was Stephen Foster.

Born on the Fourth of July, 1826, while the neighborhood was celebrating the fiftieth anniversary of the birth of our Republic, on the day when Adams and Jefferson ended their lives in its service, he seems destined from the start to make his contribution to this country.

"There is always something perfectly original about Stephen" wrote his adoring mother to one of her other eight children, but she was puzzled to know where it might find its expression. When, at the age of 13, he composed a waltz for a quartette of flutes, she might have suspected that music was his forte. But those were the days when practically the only music known to people west of the Alleghenies was that of the minstrels and the music halls; when music was not considered among the manly callings but was regarded as a pastime only, for those who had nothing better to do.

Selecting the Swanee River from the Atlas because it fitted his rhythm, he put it into a class with the Rhine and the Danube as rivers celebrated in song. It was not until after he had composed "*Old Kentucky Home,*" "*Oh, Susannah!,*" "*Old Black Joe,*" "*Massah's in de Cold, Cold Ground,*" "*Oh, Boys, Carry Me Along*" and more than a hundred others that he saw the plantation life of which he had sung. A few years later he went to New York, where in poverty and obscurity he died at the age of 38.

His was a life ineffective, unhappy and, some say, dissolute, and yet he remains, because of a handful of songs expressing universal longing and loneliness, far more famous than his father who was twice mayor of Allegheny City, and his brother who built up the Pennsylvania Railroad. "The Little White Cottage" in Pittsburgh where he spent his childhood has been preserved as a memorial, plans for a monumental Music Pavilion at the University of Pittsburgh are in work, and three of the pianos which are said to have aided him in his composing are enshrined in as many museums to testify that America is grateful that Stephen Foster lived to write its songs.

A de Borodin

Alexander Porfyrievich Borodin

"PHOTOGRAPHER OF THE RUSSIAN SOUL IN MUSIC"

[Born 1834—Died 1887]

FEW people can serve two masters at once with equal zeal; Borodin was one man who could and did. He studied medicine so assiduously that he distinguished himself both in practice and research; and at the same time he became an excellent musician. Before he was sixteen, he had learned to play the piano, violin, cello, and other instruments, and to compose, as well.

He was Russian to the marrow. Born in St. Petersburg November 12, 1834, the illegitimate son of a Georgian prince, he spent his life, except for a few concert tours, in his native land. His appointment, at the age of twenty-eight, as lecturer at the St. Petersburg Medical Academy freed him from worry about a livelihood, and enabled him to devote more and more of his energies to music.

Five musical birds of a feather flocked together, calling themselves "the Five,"—César Cui, Moussorgsky, Rimsky-Korsakov, Balakirev, and Borodin. All were pledged to save Russian music from the baleful German influence of Liszt and his colleagues. Borodin, under the inspiration of Balakirev, produced two magnificent symphonies and part of a third, an opera, a symphonic sketch, some chamber music, and a number of fine songs. An ideally happy marriage with another pianist, Mlle. Protopova, proved an additional source of inspiration.

The years 1869–72 were such crowded ones that hard work actually undermined his health. Besides his professional duties at the Medical Academy, the writing of several scientific works, and the organization of a new Medical School for Women, he was constantly composing. His opera ballet *Mlada* is of this period.

This union of science and music gave a fundamental sanity and clarity to everything he wrote, quite different from the unrestrained outpourings of some of his neurotic compatriots. He held up a musical mirror to the Russian soul so skilfully that all its essential beauty, its yearnings and strivings and disappointments were therein reflected.

His death occurred on February 28, 1887, as the finale to a triumphant piano tour of Germany with César Cui. On his return to St. Petersburg, he wrote to his wife, in Moscow, "To-morrow we have a musical party here. It will be very grand, but I must not unveil its mysteries." But when the party was at its height, while he was laughing and chatting with his friends, he suddenly collapsed,—and unveiled an unexpected mystery, the mystery of death.

Modeste Moussorgsky

"A RUSSIAN REALIST"

[Born 1835—Died 1881]

THE first decade of his life having been spent close to the soil in his native village of Karevo, where he was born on March 28, 1835, Moussorgsky returned repeatedly for inspiration to the moujik he understood so well. Yet his life had as many phases as that of the hero of a Pushkin novel.

We see him, after his schooldays, a handsome young man in the slick uniform of the Prebroaiensky Regiment, whose manicured fingers could perform wonders of improvisation on the piano, to the "Oh's" and "Ah's" of admiring ladies—an amateur among amateurs.

We see him, later, at the home of Dargomisky, awakening to the "real musical life" with such friends as Balakirev, Cui, Rimsky-Korsakov, Borodin —the powerful coterie in musical Russia. One writer calls him a cuckoo in the nest of these singing birds, for his untaught song is crude, powerful, original, unlike their polished utterances. His ambition to bring music into the closest relation to actual living made him discredit the need for intensive musical training. Never would he submit to it, lest his originality thereby be impaired.

When, in 1857, he resigns his army commission to devote himself to music, he launches upon a struggle with poverty by which he is eventually worsted. For a few years he lives with Rimsky-Korsakov who polishes and edits his orchestrations. But when the latter marries, he takes to drink and drugs to relieve his depression. The fop becomes an epileptic sloven in a dirty dressing-gown. A minor government office which he discharges with meticulous indifference, supplies absolute necessities and leaves him many hours free for composition.

When *Boris Godounoff*, his greatest opera, is produced in 1868, César Cui damns it in the *News* with such faint praise that Moussorgsky bitterly calls his friends "soulless traitors." And so they prove to be for, when the poor besotted composer dies, March 28, 1881, on his forty-sixth birthday, a charity patient in the military hospital of St. Nicholas, they are not beside him, but appear to do him tardy homage at his funeral.

The delicate children's cycle *In the Nursery*, beloved of Liszt; the sombre *No Sunlight* and *Songs and Dances of Death*, completely expressive of the dismal depths of the Russian soul; the super-realistic opera *Boris Godounoff*, huge, crude, flooded with passion and madness; *Khovantshina*, with its stirring prelude of national airs; the piano suite *In a Picture Gallery* all demonstrate Moussorgsky's pre-eminence as a song writer, his gift for realistic differentiation of character, his originality of expression, his deeply national feeling, his ability to depict life in music.

Nikolai Rimsky-Korsakov
"ONE RUSSIAN WHO DARED WRITE HAPPY MUSIC"
[Born 1844—Died 1908]

FROM navy to notation is a step for a psychological seven-league boot, especially when one is more than twenty-seven years old. But Rimsky-Korsakov, like the legendary heroes upon whom he fondly dwelt in his music, won fame, fortune and his loved one by abandoning the sea for his chosen work,—music.

Born of aristocratic parents in Petrograd March 18, 1844, he took up piano and violoncello, as every youngster of his caste did, merely as a pleasing accomplishment. His education completed, he fitted neatly into a naval uniform and naval duties. But in his free time, spent with his friends, Cui, Moussorgsky, Borodin and Balakirev, he became so passionately imbued with their idea of creating a national Russian music, that he had no thought for anything else, least of all the navy.

Thanks to the discipline of those years, he filled in the gaps in his musical education so thoroughly that in 1871 he became professor of composition in Petrograd University, directed numerous concerts, became inspector of marine bands—an echo from his navy days—and took pen in hand for a steady flow of compositions. His marriage with Nadejda Pourgold, concert pianist, united her talent and her passion for a national music with his own.

His folk-tale operas, *The Maid of Pskov, The Snow Maiden, Mlada, Sadko, The Tsar's Bride, Tsar Saltan, Kastchei the Immortal, Le Coq d'Or*, to name a few, derive from the inexhaustible storehouse of Russian legend. The "program-music" suites for orchestra, *Antar, Russian Easter, Scheherezade*, are a kaleidoscope of gay bandanas, tambourines, colored Easter eggs, and Arabian Nights' dreams. His orchestration of *Boris Godounoff*, and other unfinished works of Moussorgsky, was a tardy but ineffective tribute to the friend whose genius was as powerfully crude as his own was polished and suave. He turned toward the public only the bright side of that Russian picture whose reverse Tschaikowsky and Moussorgsky so pitilessly exposed.

Although his later years were saddened by intrigues which deprived him for a while of his position at the Conservatory, his last opera, *Le Coq d'Or*, was as full of dash and humor as any of those written in happier days. He had the satisfaction of seeing it performed, despite opposition to its supposed political ironies, before asthma and angina pectoris caused his death on June 21, 1908.

eg. Tschaikovsky.

Peter Ilitch Tschaikowsky

"SYMPHONIC APOSTLE OF GLOOM"

[Born 1840—Died 1893]

A COMBINATION of epilepsy with extreme sensitivity and emotional intensity,—and no evidence of music,—was this composer's heritage from the parents who gave him birth in Petrograd on May 7, 1840. Not an ideal equipment for a lawyer, one would say, nevertheless, he dutifully was graduated from the School of Jurisprudence at twenty-one, accepted a position in the Ministry of Justice, and enjoyed music in a purely amateur fashion.

But one day when he and his cousin were at the piano, he was struck by the latter's chord-modulations from one key to another, and nothing would satisfy him but that his parents permit him, too, to study harmony. A five-year course at Petrograd Conservatory under Nikolai Rubinstein, for which his excessive zeal induced him to write as an exercise as many as two hundred variations on a single theme, resulted in his appointment as professor of harmony at Moscow University.

All his early compositions were operas, all bad, but he persisted. The *Oprichnik*, written at thirty-four, was the first success to win him recognition in Russia. It won him, too, a tragedy, in the unsought affection of a young woman, Antonia Milyukova, who boldly proposed marriage. In all chivalry, he consented, and actually went through with it, only to flee to Switzerland within a few weeks vowing distractedly never to return.

A year later, a sadder and a wiser man, he resumed his teaching in Moscow. Fortunately, he was relieved of financial anxiety by a wealthy widow, Frau von Meck, who settled on him an annuity which enabled him to devote himself wholly to composition. His letters to this "incomparable friend" whom he never met personally, reveal in words, as his music in harmonies, the sensitive, morbid, yet loving and generous soul of their writer.

Six splendid symphonies, the symphonic fantasia *Francesca da Rimini*, *Manfred*, many operas including *Pique Dame* and *Eugen Onégin*, chamber music, one violin and several piano concertos were the products of his Russian genius plus his German training, if not purely national in technic of expression, wholly so in spirit. Especially the Sixth, or *Pathetic Symphony*, is one long, magnificently orchestrated sob.

Its depression may have been prophetic, for almost as soon as it was completed, Tschaikowsky contracted cholera from drinking unboiled water while an epidemic was raging in Moscow. He had several times attempted suicide, and now finally, on November 6, 1893, Nature granted him his wish to die. Thus passed the most freely expressive composer of the romantic school in Russia.

Edvard Grieg

Edvard Hagerup Grieg

"THE CHOPIN OF THE NORTH"

[Born 1843—Died 1907]

*T*HE eyes of Edvard Grieg mirrored in their cool, fjord-green depths not only his own soul but the whole soul of his people, and as he cast them upon the music he wrote, their peculiar national radiance lingered there and became a part of it, giving it a limpid charm that is at once personal and universal.

Trolls and pixies and bearded mountain kings peopled the tales told him during his happy childhood in Bergen, where he was born June 15, 1843. The German teacher in school who dismissed as trash the theme with variations which Edvard handed him one day in lieu of a boring German essay, was his bad genie even as Ole Bull, the friendly violinist, was his good one. Fortunately the latter won out, so that Edvard, who had already had a good musical grounding from his mother, was sent to study, first at the Leipsic Conservatory, and then to Christiania where Niels Gade encouraged his early efforts.

With his friend Richard Nordraak, he established the Euterpe Society in Christiania, the members of which solemnly vowed to do all in their power to further the development of national music. Nina Hagerup, Edvard's cousin, was one of the supporters who most nobly lived up to her pledge by marrying him and singing his songs inimitably when, together, they made concert tours of Germany, England, France, Holland and Denmark. The ocean trip to America was too strenuous an undertaking for this frail Viking who suffered and eventually died of tuberculosis, but the honors heaped upon him abroad had their repercussions in the increasing popularity of his works here.

The *Peer Gynt Suite*, tale of a Scandinavian Rip Van Winkle, whose youth is dissipated in carousals with the monsters in the Hall of the Mountain King, while his wife and his mother vainly await his return, is melodious, colorful program music, written when ill-health had forced his retirement to the quiet of his villa outside Bergen. By this time he had produced many songs, in which dances, used as themes, were developed with grace, rhythm and delicacy. Leaving symphonic writing to more heroic men, his music is no more robust than was he, but equally charming, sincere and individual.

The villa, Troldhaugen, where he died September 5, 1907, is venerated as the shrine of Norwegian music.

Arthur Sullivan

Sir Arthur Sullivan

"A BRITISH PEER OF SONG"

[Born 1842—Died 1900]

THE red and gold of Sullivan's uniform as chorister of the Chapel Royal was no more brilliant than his career. Born in London May 13, 1842, of highly intelligent parents, the curly-headed, mischievous lad who was to become the idol of England first exercised his musical lung-power on the wind instruments of his father's military band, then in singing hymns at the Chapel Royal. "Onward, Christian soldiers," outstanding among the many hymns he published later in his career, is grateful tribute to his early training.

Having won the Mendelssohn scholarship, he went for a year's study to Leipsic, "discovered" the music of Schumann and Schubert, and came back to England humming it along with his own cantata, *The Tempest*, to win immediate popularity for both. *The Kenilworth Cantata*, *Irish Symphony*, and *In Memoriam Overture* are other serious works, but it was the light operas he wrote with his witty collaborator, W. S. Gilbert, that brought him fame and fortune.

All fashionable London descended to the dingy underground theatre where their first attempts were given, and followed them thence to the Savoy Theatre, built to house their productions fittingly. During the twenty-five years when one was flint to the other's steel, they wrote *Trial by Jury*, *Patience*, *Pinafore*, *The Pirates of Penzance*, *Iolanthe*, *The Gondoliers*, *Yeomen of the Guard* and many more. *The Mikado*, probably most popular of all, was written after Sullivan had tearfully protested to Gilbert that "he could write no more, his inspiration was completely exhausted." Nevertheless, the wit of the words, the tunefulness of the music, the complete suitability of each to the other in this, as in the rest of these operettas, had never before been equaled. On a "first night" at the Savoy, the enthusiasts in the gallery would sing, under an impromptu leader, hits from the other operettas, with Sullivan frequently sitting among them, although Queen Victoria had reserved a place for him in the royal box.

She it was who, by urging him unceasingly to produce a serious opera, finally killed the goose who laid such golden eggs of melody. A quarrel with Gilbert, and the eventual divorcement of their talents was the result,— the more the pity, for in the years that followed neither produced anything further of value, either separately, or in a last feeble attempt to renew their collaboration.

Sullivan died of cancer, November 22, 1900. Fittingly sung to rest in Westminster Abbey by the choristers of the Chapel Royal, he died as he had lived, in a blaze of red and gold and glory.

Johannes Brahms

"THE PHILOSOPHER OF MUSIC"

[Born 1833—Died 1897]

THE best-known picture of Brahms shows him seated at the piano, a fat cigar between his lips, a fat abdomen between him and the keyboard, his pockets bulging, his whole personality from the Santa Claus beard to the baggy trousers exuding comfort, geniality, and contentment. And such was his nature in later life.

His first twenty years in Hamburg were years of rigid discipline. His father, a contrabass player in the theatre orchestra, could barely support the family, and Brahms did all manner of odd jobs to help, from blacking boots to playing in his father's traveling band and music halls and peddling his own melodies. But whatever else he did, his regular schooling and his study of music went steadily forward.

Opportunity knocked when Reményi, the Hungarian violinist, took the twenty-year-old boy on tour as accompanist. Through Reményi, he not only learned the gypsy melodies later incorporated in the *Hungarian Dances*, but also met Joachim and Liszt, valuable friends to him in later years.

Schumann, however, was the friend whose accolade knighted him. When Brahms came to Leipsic, he hailed him as a prophet, writer of music "the like of which he never had heard before." His articles in musical journals drew attention to the young man's work, his encouragement spurred him to effort, his home, with its charming presiding genius, Klara Schumann, was always open to him. This friendship was touchingly repaid by Brahms' devotion to Klara during Schumann's illness and after his death.

A few ideal years of teaching and composing at the court of Lippe-Detmold, several more in Hamburg, and we see him a mature genius. It was in Vienna that his later life was lived,—the centre where all the mighty in music, literature and art foregathered. From 1862 until his death, April 3, 1897, he held his place,—no inconsiderable one,—in that circle. He never married, saying, "It is as hard to marry as to write an opera. Perhaps in both a first success might embolden one to try again, but it wants more courage than mine to make a start."

His music stands beside that of Bach and Beethoven. To their classic line he has added all the flexibility and richness of modern instrumentation, sacrificing none of the essential simplicity of melody. Four glorious symphonies, orchestral pieces, such as the *Academic Festival Overture* and the *Tragic Overture*, chamber-music, instrumental music, 230 songs of unique beauty, among them, "*Die Mainacht*," "*Feldeinsamkeit*," "*Das Wiegenlied*," and "*O Wüsst ich doch den Weg Zurück*," are his contribution. To know them, as to know their writer, is to love them.

Richard Strauss

"A ROMANTIC REALIST"

[*Born 1864—*   ]

NO FATHER ever gave his son a more complete kit of tools for his trade than the elder Strauss, a distinguished horn player, bestowed upon his son, Richard. Born in Munich on June 11, 1864, he was taught to read his notes before his letters; to play the piano at four; to compose as naturally as he talked. His equipment included, as well, a full set of prejudices against all so-called modern ideas, especially Wagner's. All the tricks of the orchestral trade which he had at his fingertips when he left Munich University at twenty were vowed to the perpetuation of the classic ideals of Mozart and Beethoven.

But he had a friend, Alexander Ritter, who led him, if not astray, then away from the classic, through the flowery paths of program music and so to realism. A chance hearing of *Tristan und Isolde* reduced him to apologetic raptures and caused him to write his first symphonic poem, *Aus Italien*, on an ensuing trip. Eight others followed—*Macbeth, Don Juan, Death and Transfiguration, Til Eulenspiegel, Thus Spake Zarathustra, The Hero, Don Quixote* and the *Domestic Symphony*. All are so eloquently expressive that the accompanying program notes are hardly required. Strauss is said to have remarked that "music was becoming such a definite art that we should soon be able to portray a tablespoon so unmistakably that it could be told from the rest of the silverware." The marvelous characterizations of his own music, with the smashing dishes and crying babies of the symphony, the bleating sheep and creaking windmills of *Don Quixote*, etc., ably support that extreme statement.

But now the opera beckoned. *Rosenkavalier, Salome, Elektra* and *The Egyptian Helen* are products of his third or realistic period of composition. They range in mood from the airy waltz romance of *Rosenkavalier* to the plangent dissonances of *Salome*. Their frankness at first laid them open to the charge of vulgarity, but as realism in music has come to be increasingly admired, their success in that realm has silenced their critics. Beautiful songs and choruses, chamber-music and two symphonies complete the list of his works.

The blond, blue-eyed giant of immaculate appearance has played the piano, conducted, and collected honors and degrees all over the world, including America. But he loves best a glass of beer and a game of cards in his own home, with the wife he married, characteristically, after hearing her sing Elizabeth in *Tannhäuser* when he conducted it at Bayreuth. Here he has continued composing, nothing daunted by his world-wide reputation as prince of program-music makers and first of the moderns.

Claudio Jean Antonio Monteverdi

"FIRST OF THE GREAT OPERA COMPOSERS"

[Born 1567—Died 1643]

EVEN while a student of music with his master, Ingegneri, in Cremona, where he was born in May, 1567, young Monteverdi had the courage to question the rigid rules of counterpoint which were rammed down his throat. And when he dutifully wrote the madrigals that were expected of him, publishing his first book when he was sixteen and three others before he was forty, he slyly took liberties with the primitive models, making use of harmonic progressions and discords and repeated notes, devices which presaged his later startling innovations in the field of opera.

It was at the liberal court of Vincenzo, Duke of Gonzaga, in Mantua, that Monteverdi, with Tasso, Galileo, and other free-thinkers began in earnest to develop his own ideas. He saw the world with his restless patron, whom he accompanied on his travels, now to battle, now in the pursuit of culture, and learned much thereby.

When he was forty, at the command of Vincenzo, he wrote his first opera, *Orfeo*, followed a year later by *Arianna*, with its famous lamentation "Lasciatemi morire." Their success emboldened him to write others, of which two are outstanding, *Ritorno d'Ulisse* and *Incoronazione di Poppea*, the latter classed as the "greatest opera of the seventeenth century." In them, and in his church writings also, Monteverdi continually stressed emotional expression, in contrast to the "reverent ecstasy" of earlier writings.

Although he did not originate the lyric drama, he imposed strange alterations upon the form of Peri's *Euridice*, the accepted model. He introduced the recitativo, chanted by the solo voice with orchestral accompaniment. He assigned parts to individual choirs in the orchestra, creating a kind of crude polyphony, noisy, but novel enough to win him the title of fountainhead of modern orchestration. When he tried to explain the tremolo effect to his violinists, so the story goes, they refused to play anything so outlandish as the same note repeated sixteen times in rapid succession, unable to see why one long note would not answer equally as well. They received the suggestion of pizzicato, or plucking the strings, with equal uneasiness. These, and all of his new tricks, were designed to one end,— increased emotional expressiveness.

His ideas continued to flow with undiminished freshness until his death on November 29, 1643, at which time, aged seventy-six, he was just trying out the cantata, a new song-form. Modern opera composers down to Wagner have followed the stormy lead of this sixteenth century pioneer.

Pergolesi

Giovanni Battista Pergolesi

"ITALY'S SPOILED DARLING"

[Born 1710—Died 1736]

ONE of the lesser stars whose light twinkled for fewer than the al-
lotted span of years was Pergolesi. Since, like the poet, Keats,
he died of tuberculosis before he was thirty, there is more of promise
than of performance in the works he left. Still, the list is not inconsiderable,
comprising twelve operas, three oratorios, a number of masses, cantatas and
other church music, thirty trios and the famous *Stabat Mater*.

Romance colors his life. Born of obscure parents in the tiny town of
Jesi, on January 10, 1710, he grew his musical wings in the Conservatorio
dei Poveri, in Naples. His instinctive talent for composition was noticed
when he played on the violin some chromatic passages he had written, and
thereafter he became the petted protégé of the head of the Conservatorio.

Handsome as the painter Raphael whom he closely resembled, courted
right and left after the success of his first opera, *San Guglielmo d'Aquitania*,
(1731), he had every inducement to riotous living, inducements to which
he succumbed freely, his excesses being notable even in those tolerant days.

But at the première of his last opera, *L'Olimpiade*, cat-calls and rotten
oranges were the response of the fickle Italians who had so generously
applauded his earlier efforts. As he sat bowed in discouragement, a titled
lady, Maria Spinelli, quieted the hubbub and whispered a few words of
cheer. A mutual love grew from the incident, waxing ever more ardent
until the day when Maria's three brothers marched in, armed to the teeth,
and offered her the choice between marrying a man of her own rank or
seeing her lover slain. She chose to retire to a convent where she died
within the year.

Pergolesi, meanwhile, racked by consumption, betook himself to
Pozzuoli, where he composed his last and greatest piece, the *Stabat Mater*, a
tribute to his love. Passionate and dramatic, it is operatic rather than
religious music, but it has distinct sentimental charm. Bellini called it a
"divina poema del dolore." Shortly after it was completed, March 16,
1736, its composer breathed his last.

His best opera, *La Serva Padrona*, one of the first Italian operas to be
recognized in Paris long after its composer was beyond hearing, precipitated
the famous anti-Rameau controversy in 1752, wherein Rameau's supremacy
in the opera was first challenged. Its vivacious, sparkling dialogue was
a blessed relief from the stilted operatic grandiloquence then in vogue.
Pergolesi was ahead of his time in spirit; his influence was the yeast that
lightened the musical dough of many of his successors.

Christoph Willibald Gluck
"GERMAN FATHER OF FRENCH OPERA"
[Born 1714—Died 1787]

A RECORD of more than twenty operas, all bad, before his fortieth year, could hardly be called a glowing start for the Father of the Opera, as Gluck came to be known. But in the course of time he retrieved himself from the reputation given him by Handel who said: "He knows no more counterpoint than mein cook!" by raising himself to the summit of success as opera composer par excellence to two empresses.

Son of a Bavarian gamekeeper, born near Nuremberg, on the 2nd of July, 1714, he received rare preparation for the amenities of court life, first in a Jesuit school, where he picked up much philosophy, history and science, in addition to some musical training, then on travels with various noble patrons. During the ten years he conducted the opera in Vienna he gave music lessons to the little Princess Marie Antoinette, who so loved the gruff German, never gruff with her, that almost her first act, when she became queen, was to summon Gluck to her court at Versailles in 1774.

By this time he had already produced *The Shepherd King, Orpheus and Euridice, Alceste* and *Paris and Helen.* Characterized by an extreme simplicity, compared with florid Italian models, they drove even Rousseau to the unwilling admission that "opera could be sung in French."

All the support his friends could give him was needed when, in 1776, a rival composer, the Italian Piccini, was pitted against him in a contest to determine which was the better man of music. *Le Coin du Roi* (Italian) argued with *Le Coin de la Reine* (French) and not until both men had submitted operas on the same subject, *Iphigenia in Tauris* and Gluck's had been acclaimed superior, did the excitement die down. It left him more popular than ever. His innovations, such as the introduction of the overture, the subordination of vocal gymnastics to musical effects, the enrichment of the orchestra by adding cymbals and kettle-drum, and the increasing of its importance as accompaniment to the voice, were all accepted. *Iphigenia in Aulis,* written in 1774, and *Armide,* three years later, completed the list of seven operas in the style of simple grandeur upon which his fame rests.

"If the Greeks had had a musician, they would have had Gluck" it has been said. Unfortunately, not the Greeks, but the French had him, and what with wining and dining and excesses from which not even his good wife, Marianne Pergin, could deter him, he grew heavier and more choleric, until a stroke carried him off on November 15, 1787.

Carl Maria von Weber

Carl Maria von Weber

"FORE-RUNNER OF WAGNER"

[*Born 1786—Died 1826*]

THE talent of Carl Maria von Weber was a bud so brutally forced by an ambitious father that its blossoming was truly a miracle. A double heritage of tuberculosis from his young mother and the prodigy tradition from Mozart, husband of his Aunt Constance, darkened his early years almost from the moment of his birth in Eutin, Germany, December 18, 1786. For his father formed the family into a group of strolling players, held Carl's baby fingers to the violin and piano when they could barely grasp, and denied him regular education, in his greed for the profits if the boy should actually develop into a child wonder. When he was twelve, his mother who, in her feeble way, had shielded the lame, sensitive child from the father's evil influence, died.

By the time he was eighteen, Carl knew all there was to know about stage life, including its profligacies. A period of riotous dissipation as secretary to the Prince of Württemberg resulted in his exile with his precious father. But he did not mend his ways, even when entrusted with the responsibility of leading, first the Prague, then the Dresden Opera. Instead, he plunged ever deeper into an affair with the disreputable Theresa Brunetti, which bade fair to ruin him as conductor, composer, and man. In the nick of time a good angel, the singer Caroline Brandt, rescued him, married him, and helped him to settle down to composing those great operas, masterpieces of the German romantic school, which have placed him securely among the immortals.

When the gay *Invitation to the Dance*, and music from *Der Freischütz*, *Euryanthe*, and *Oberon* are played, they are always the signal for heads to wag and feet to tap in delighted rhythm with the familiar strains. The supernatural stories they relate, the transformation of traditional operatic lay-figures into flesh-and-blood by the use of Leitmotifs, a device commonly credited entirely to Wagner, the treatment of the orchestra as an integral element in music-drama, painting in tones the stage picture, the realization of new color-possibilities in the use of flute, bassoon, oboe, and clarinet, put these works in the relation of first cousin, if not even closer, to the music dramas of Wagner and his successors.

He journeyed to England, mastered the language, and wrote *Oberon* all within a few months, to his undoing, for his end was hastened by this over-exertion, and he died at forty, murmuring "I want to go home."

G. Rossini

Gioacchino Antonio Rossini

"A COMPOSER IN SPITE OF HIMSELF"

[*Born 1792—Died 1868*]

MORE orders than he could fill, more money than he needed, more success than he wanted—such was the extraordinary fortune of Gioacchino Rossini, born of a pretty opera singer and of a father who was town trumpeter in Pesaro during the leap-year in which Mozart died (February 29, 1792). At the age of thirty-seven, having completed "William Tell," his thirtieth opera in fourteen years, he ceased writing altogether until the last year of his life when he wrote his famous *Stabat Mater*, preferring, as he said, the glory of inventing a new salad dressing which won the cardinal's blessing to all the fame which might come to him as composer.

Endowed with an angel's voice, he sang in churches at the age of ten. At twelve he sang in opera or played the piano which then accompanied the orchestra. At fourteen he wrote his first opera. At eighteen he had one performed at Naples, and at twenty another at La Scala in Milan—the climax of any opera-composer's career.

Marrying his leading-lady, Isabella Colbran, he spent the next few years travelling about Europe, writing to order only and under such great pressure that the pages of his manuscripts often went straight from his pen to the conductor's stand. Everywhere he was the rage; even the arrival of Napoleon himself in the same town could not quench the *tutto furore* which accompanied his presence. "There need be no ceremony between emperors," said the little Corsican when they met. After singing duets with King George IV in London, is it astonishing that he set himself up as autocrat of musical Paris, wielding great influence, even as he did in Italy, where Donizetti and Bellini flattered him with their imitations?

The *opera bouffe* he converted into comedies, such as *Il Barbiere di Siviglia* and *La Gazza Ladra*, and to the *opera seria* he gave new energy with his *Tancred*, *Semiramis* and others. Many innovations, which suggest Italian opera to the lay mind, are ascribed to him, such as the introduction of the brass band and the ardent prayer; the instrumental accompaniment of the recitative which Monteverdi used so freely, and the *crescendo*, that mounting augmentation of sound to a climax.

Adelina Patti, Christine Nilsson and Alboni sang at his funeral. His fortune he dedicated to the establishment of the "Foundation Rossini" in Paris where musicians may be as lazy as they like in their old age—his own idea of heaven and earth.

Donizetti

Gaetano Donizetti

"A MANUFACTURER OF OPERAS"

[Born 1797—Died 1848]

*L*IKE the one-hoss shay, in comparison with the Rolls-Royce, Donizetti's old-fashioned operas have for music-lovers today a charm that is more floridly historic than musically appealing. He wrote so quickly and fluently, with a shrewd eye cocked upon the barometer of public opinion, that his facile output escapes lasting fame by its very volume.

His father, a weaver, ambitiously destined him for the law from the moment when he uttered his first wail, in Bergamo, Italy, November 25, 1797. But he continued wailing as soon as he learned of the profession that had been selected for him, even going to the length of donning a uniform to escape the woolsack. First, however, he persuaded his father to let him study harmony with Padre Matteu, in the nearby town of Bologna, using church music, to his parent's annoyance, as a stepping-stone to the stage.

His army career was enlivened by the production of one opera after another, until in 1822 his *Zoraïde de Granada* so captivated the public that they carried him in triumph through the streets of Rome, crowning him with laurel on the steps of the Capitol itself. His honorable discharge from the army followed inevitably.

Both he and his friend Bellini were pupils and imitators of the greater Rossini, and in the thirty operas Donizetti reeled off prior to 1832, there is no touch of originality. But the seven that survive of his total output of seventy—*La Fille du Régiment, Don Pasquale, Lucia di Lammermoor, L'Elisir d'Amore, Lucrezia Borgia, La Favorita* and *Linda*—have graceful, vivacious melodies, brilliant if somewhat disconnected solos, and a certain dramatic power that are characteristic.

His facility he evinced by writing the operetta *Il Campanella di Notte* in one week's time, in order to save a tottering opera company from bankruptcy. The fourth act of *La Favorita* he composed in four hours, when the friend with whom he was dining went out to a party leaving Donizetti over the coffee-cups, and returned at midnight to find him still there, eager to sing the aria he had just finished.

Concert tours, his work as director of various conservatories, and constant composition wore him out. Paralyzed and insane during his last years, he greeted visitors with the startling announcement, "Poor Donizetti is dead." On April 8, 1848, his anticipatory statement was realized.

Giuseppe Verdi

"KING OF ITALIAN OPERA"

[*Born 1813—Died 1901*]

PERHAPS the only violent act of Giuseppe Verdi's serene life was to smash the spinet on which the village priest was teaching him to play, when it failed to reproduce the chord he wanted. That was when he was a very small boy in Bereto, Parma, where he was born October 13, 1813. An acolyte in the village church when the smashing took place, a few years later he was playing flute and clarinet in the cathedral, and at eleven became organist. He received never more than fifty cents monthly for these services, which he performed conscientiously, although he had daily to plod three miles each way to and from school at Busseto. Finally, however, his townspeople rewarded his talent and industry by presenting him with a scholarship under Saletti, in Milan.

His opera, *Oberto*, composed in 1838 in the first flush of happiness after his marriage, so impressed Mirelli, impresario at La Scala, that he enthusiastically commissioned Verdi to write three more, the first a comedy. But alas! A fever which carried off his wife and two babies transformed the comedy into a tragedy, and a failure. It was several distracted years before the friendly insistence of Mirelli induced him to try again.

Nabuco, produced in 1842, was notable chiefly because he married its prima donna, Giuseppina Strepponi. *I Lombardi* and *Attila*, which contains the rousing song "Thou shalt have the universe, let Italy be mine" made of him a national hero hardly less potent in politics than in music.

More tunes from *Ernani*, *Rigoletto*, *La Traviata*, *Il Trovatore*, *Un Ballo in Maschera*, *La Forza del Destino* have been ground out by street-organs and whistled by a public unconscious of their source than any other melodies in two decades. *Aïda*, commissioned by the Khedive of Egypt, and produced on an imperial scale with live elephants and all the trappings of state, made operatic history in the magnificence of its production as well as its music.

The grand old man of Italian opera, like fine wine, mellowed as he aged. In his later works,—the stately *Requiem Mass* for Manzoni, and the operas *Aïda*, *Otello*, and *Falstaff*, his flowing melodies are enriched by an increased command of the resources of the orchestra, possibly in response to Wagner's influence, to be imitated in its turn by subsequent Italian opera composers.

When, on January 27, 1901, he died peacefully in his villa, he, like Rossini, left instructions dedicating to the support of less successful confrères the fortune of his making.

Gounod

Charles Gounod
"THE IDOL OF FRENCH OPERA"
[Born 1818—Died 1893]

WHEN the Director of the Paris Opera was asked recently to name the most popular French opera of today, he unhesitatingly replied, "Gounod's *Faust*." And yet this melodious setting of Goethe's epic was closed after a four month's run in 1859 at the Théatre Lyrique in Paris, the Opéra Comique having refused to take it and no publisher having been found willing to gamble on printing the score. It was not until ten years later, after a total of 300 successful performances outside of France, that it finally landed in the repertoire of the Paris Opera.

Born in Paris, June 17, 1818, Charles Gounod evinced his talent at an early age. His mother, an artist, did her best to make a practical man of him, but he went his way on the usual composer's course—Conservatoire, Prix de Rome, a year abroad. The music of Palestrina, heard in Rome, so developed his native piety that, on his return, he seriously contemplated the priesthood and adopted the title of Abbé Gounod.

It was thanks to the frivolous influence of his friends, Fanny Mendelssohn and Pauline Viardot, that he turned his back to the church and his talents to the composition of opera. *Sapho*, his first, was in some ways ahead of its time. But it was in *Faust* and *Romeo and Juliette* that he made his contribution of a style which mercifully does away with the gymnastics of Rossini and dares to be fresh, simple, tender and expressive. His beautiful melody and masterly orchestration have served as models for writers of modern French opera even in *La Reine de Saba*, *Philemon and Baucis* and *Le Médecin Malgré Lui*, not generally regarded as his greatest works.

Like Handel he spent a number of years in London, trying, among other things, to duplicate his early *Mass of St. Cécile* and succeeding with two great pieces, *The Redemption* and *Death in Life*. Ardent, expansive, amiable, happy and sincere, he merited the petting he received at the fair hands of the English ladies who clustered as devotedly about him as did their French sisters.

At seventy-five, crippled and blinded by a paralytic stroke, he composed a *Requiem*, heard it played and, as he reached forward to place it in his cabinet, fell over, unconscious, and died. This was on the 13th of October, 1893. Hosts of admirers, sworn to be his musical disciples, followed him to his grave at Saint Cloud.

Georges Alexandre Bizet

"HE PROVED QUALITY TO BE MORE ENDURING THAN QUANTITY"

[Born 1838—Died 1875]

THE thirty-seven years of Georges Bizet's life flowered in one grand opera, *Carmen*. He wrote others, but this alone lives on, and has been called the one perfect opera.

He went through the usual routine training of a composer. He was born in Bougival, near Paris, October 25, 1838, the son of a teacher of singing. At ten, he embarked upon the course at the Paris Conservatoire, and nine years later, when he was graduated, he carried off the Prix de Rome for his cantata, *Chloris et Clotilde*. The same year, his operetta, *Docteur Miracle*, now forgotten, was awarded the prize in a contest sponsored by Offenbach.

After his three years in Rome, he returned to Paris to teach, play the piano, compose, and enjoy a happy married life with the daughter of Halévy, his teacher at the Conservatoire. But his operas were coldly received, because of some real or fancied resemblance in their orchestration to that of Wagner, who was then being emphatically hissed from every stage in Paris.

Even *Carmen* had to win a difficult way to recognition, although in enumerating its virtues it is difficult to see why. The libretto, taken from a popular novel by Prosper Merimée, was cleverly written, with full emphasis on the dramatic interest of the story of the fascinating cigarette girl and her two lovers, one of whom loved her to his own undoing, and to hers. The music was highly colorful and magnificently orchestrated, with new elements in the use of flute and harp in the orchestra. There were many melodies to catch an audience.

And yet Bizet, when d'Indy praised his work during the entr'acte of the first performance, said gloomily, "You are the first who has said that, and I fancy you will be the last." He left the performance, not humming the Toreador song, but with tears in his eyes, convinced that yet another failure had been scored against him.

Three months later, with *Carmen* scheduled for performance in Vienna, and with repeated performances being given in Paris, he admitted that it might be called a success. But the conviction came too late. He had heart disease, and the original disappointment undoubtedly wounded his sensitive spirit, hastening his end. He died in Bougival on June 31, 1875, and never knew how many prima donnas would climb to fame in the rôle he had created for them, nor how many composers would follow *Carmen* as an operatic model, nor how many audiences in all parts of the world would hail it as their favorite opera.

J. Massenet

Jules Massenet

"WHO WROTE OPERAS FOR PRIMA DONNAS"

[Born 1842—Died 1912]

ASKED when he found time for composing in a heavy schedule of teaching at the Conservatoire, which began at seven in the morning, Massenet replied: "When *you* sleep!" Industry, concentration and a well-organized existence characterized this composer, whose life was dedicated to his music and to the France he served as a soldier during the Franco-Prussian War.

Born in Montaud, May 12, 1842, he was fortunate in having his family move to Paris, when he was eleven, that he might study at the Conservatoire. So happy was he there that, when they moved away, two years later, he ran back to Paris repeatedly until he had persuaded them that he had best remain there, which he did until, at the age of twenty-one, he won the Prix de Rome. He derived much inspiration for his compositions from his travels in the musical circles of Austria, Hungary, Bohemia and Germany— not the least valuable emoluments of the Prix.

Even before he began writing operas he had already attracted attention with oratorios and concert pieces, but it was not until he composed *Marie Magdeleine* in 1872, an oratorio-drama, that he won the praise of Tschaikowsky, St. Saëns and Gounod. In the eighteen years while he was teaching counterpoint at the Conservatoire to such men as Charpentier, Pierné, and Leroux, he produced more than a dozen operas whose titles are inalienably associated with the names of the prima donnas for whom they were written: Sybil Sanderson in *Esclarmonde;* Marie Heilbronn, who was lured from retirement with *Manon;* Lucy Arbell in *Don Quixote*, *Bacchus* and *Roma;* Marie Rénard, the original Charlotte in *Werther;* Lina Cavalieri in *Cherubin;* Emma Calvé in *La Navarraise* and *Sapho;* and Mary Garden who brought all these rôles to America.

Even in *Le Jongleur de Notre Dame*, composed for five male voices, it remained for Mary Garden to make a success of the title-rôle. No woman with a beautiful voice failed to receive a word of gratitude in his *Souvenirs*— "women for whom he dropped precious dots of ink on paper instead of sending them pearls from the *Rue de la Paix*" as Carl Van Vechten has said.

At his home in Égreville, where he "grew roses, pruned grape-vines, and in a red dressing-gown composed operas" while his devoted wife, Mlle. Sainte-Marie, his former pupil, hovered about him, he died at the age of seventy on August 13, 1912, a man who had lived happily, moderately and successfully.

Victor Herbert

"HE COMPOSED BY THE YARD—AND ALL GOOD"

[Born 1859—Died 1924]

BY BIRTH an Irishman; by education a German; by adoption an American; by temperament a Bohemian—that is Victor Herbert, cellist, bandleader, composer of light operas, the Play-boy of Broadway.

He was the indubitable grandson of that Samuel Lover, Irish patriot and artist with whom the Herbert grandchildren spent their early years after the death of their own father. When, later, their mother married a German doctor, Victor was sent to the Gymnasium at Stuttgart where, through an enforced performance on a piccolo in a school orchestra, his musical talent was discovered.

Not long thereafter he became so proficient with the cello that he was engaged for the orchestra of Edouard Strauss, of the Waltz-King family, to play under such guest conductors as Liszt, St. Saëns, Délibes and Brahms. While playing at the Stuttgart opera, he studied composition and met Therese Foerster, Viennese prima donna, a "find" of Walter Damrosch, the new assistant to Director Grau of the Metropolitan. Since the beautiful Foerster would not go to America without her affianced Victor Herbert, Damrosch had to engage him, also.

In his first eight years' residence in the United States he was a member of various orchestras and quartettes, and conductor of the Pittsburgh Symphony, but when he accepted the baton of the 22nd Regiment, known as Gilmore's Band, he definitely broke with serious music. Perhaps this was well, for his light operas will probably live in the musical repertoire of this country far longer than any of his other compositions, even his one serious opera, *Natoma*, produced at the Metropolitan Opera House.

If the "Gay Nineties" were gay, it was largely due to the operettas of Victor Herbert who "composed by the yard—and all good." Each is somebody's favorite: *The Wizard of the Nile; Babes in Toyland; Mlle. Modiste; The Red Mill; The Madcap Duchess; The Only Girl; Naughty Marietta* and all the rest.

It was in the midst of intense living—composing, conducting, rehearsing, relishing good food and drink—that he suddenly collapsed May 26, 1924, leaving a host of colorful memories:—the composer standing at his high desk, like a clerk in an English counting house; the bon vivant, in frock coat and topper, circling "the great thirst belt of New York"; his 250 pounds resplendent in red and gilt uniform leading his band up Fifth Avenue or playing the dance music at Mrs. Bradley Martin's famous balls—pictures which will endure as long as his operettas "with the whistle in them."

Giacomo Puccini

"THE SPORTSMAN COMPOSER"

[Born 1858—Died 1924]

A STRAIGHT-SHOULDERED, brown-eyed, bushy-haired mountaineer in yellow boots, a blouse and beret to match, dashing off in a high-powered car from his villa Torre del Lago, near the Gulf of Spezzia, with completed opera score under his arm—this was Giacomo Puccini, composer, sportsman, millionaire Bohemian.

Born December 23, 1858, child of the third generation of a family of musicians, living in the ancient walled city of Lucca, his life was uneventful until, in his nineteenth year, Queen Margherita gave him a grant for a year's study in Milan at the Reale Conservatorio di Musica. There he met Mascagni, Peccia and Trindelli, who became his inseparable companions in the Bohemian life in which they engaged with gusto and which he so enchantingly depicts in his *Capriccio Sinfonica* and his opera, *La Bohème*, based upon Murger's libretto. The quartette shared the thousand lire prize won by the *Sinfonica* to pay food bills in arrears; they went as one man to confer with librettists and publishers who had sent for Puccini alone, and they all played together in the orchestra of La Scala where Campanari and Toscanini were cellists in the same pit.

Seeking "a libretto that can move the world," he read thousands. For *Manon Lescaut*, with which he had won instant acclaim in 1893, he used the lovely story of the Abbé Prévost; and for *Tosca* the book by Sardou whom he had met in Paris where Daudet, Zola and Victorien were also numbered among his friends. *Madame Butterfly*, based upon the story of John Luther Long, was booed and hissed when it was first produced under Gatti-Casazza at La Scala in 1904, but, after considerable revision, was received with better grace. It was the Italian version, produced by Conried in New York with Farrar, Scotti, Caruso and Homer in the cast, that brought it real popularity and fame. When *The Girl of the Golden West* was put on at the Metropolitan in 1910, Puccini went to New York to supervise the production, but in spite of Toscanini's conducting, Belasco's production and Caruso's singing, it was a disappointment to his host of devoted disciples.

A lighter opera *La Rondine* (The Swallow), three short one-act operas, produced at the Metropolitan in 1918, and *Turandot* complete the list of his works. The last, scheduled for La Scala, New York and Chicago for the season of 1925, was interrupted by the composer's death on November 29, 1924, while *Butterfly* was being sung in Rome and *Bohème* at the Metropolitan. Mussolini, who had nominated him to the Italian Senate, gave him a funeral of State as befitted this composer who brought fame to Italy and millions to the opera houses which produced his works of flowing melody, vivid orchestration and infinite stage-craft.

Pietro Mascagni

"TO WHOM SUCCESS CAME TOO SUDDENLY"

[*Born December 7, 1863*   ]

WAKING up one fine morning to find himself famous, when *Cavalleria Rusticana* won a prize, was evidently a most upsetting experience for the young Pietro Mascagni for, from that day to this, he has never produced another work of musical distinction.

Beginning with the parental opposition which seems to goad so many men to success, he proved himself worthy of a musical education to an irate father who had destined him for the law, and was sent by a faithful uncle to the Conservatory at Milan where he became one of the famous quartette of whom Puccini was also a member. After a few years of making more personal history than music, he suddenly disappeared, no one knew where or why, to reappear five years later with a wife and a half-finished opera score and the confession that he had been strolling about the country with a travelling opera troupe as conductor, learning from experience about orchestration and the theatre what it had irked him to learn in the conservatory class-room.

Hearing of a competition for a one-act opera to be produced in Rome free of expense to the composer, Mascagni hurriedly prepared a score for a drama which his librettist sent him scene by scene and rushed it in at the last moment. That was in March, 1890; in May *Cavalleria Rusticana* was produced at the Costanzi Theatre in Rome, an instant success. Populace and critics hailed him as Verdi's successor and the King made him a Chevalier of the Order of the Crown of Italy, an honor not accorded his predecessor until a ripe old age. His return to the town of Leghorn, where he was born December 7, 1863, was a kind of triumphal procession, the entire population turning out to greet him in a city illuminated and decorated as for a festival. Even Wagner welcomed the crisp, refreshing quality of this little curtain-raiser which gave audiences tunes to carry home as the current, more richly orchestrated scores had not done for many years. It has never met with anything but success and popularity wherever it has been played, and has set the fashion for one-act operas ever since.

Since then there is little to record: *Iris*, a three-act opera on a Japanese theme has been produced at the Metropolitan twice in an interval of sixteen years; *Le Maschère*, produced in seven cities simultaneously and hissed off the boards in five; and, finally, *La Pinotta*, of which he conducted the première in Milan in 1932, fifty-three years after he wrote the score and presented it to his landlady in part-payment of a board-bill. The manuscript, which was found in an old trunk by her nephew, caused a flurry of excitement more sentimental than musical.

Richard Wagner

(Wilhelm) Richard Wagner

"DER MEISTERSINGER"
[Born 1813—Died 1883]

*I*T IS forbidden to discuss religion or Wagner." In 1860 thrifty German café-owners so placarded their walls and protected their china from the breakage that followed any mention of the greatest revolutionary of his day.

Born in Leipsic May 22, 1813, Wagner found himself at an early age on intimate terms with the stage, thanks to his stepfather Geyer, an actor. Having heard Beethoven's *Egmont*, and attempted an overture and a symphony, he decided at twenty-one on a musical career. Poverty, political persecution, derision, repeated failures never caused him to swerve from his self-appointed task of creating operas with a dramatic story, and with an orchestral part equal, if not superior to, the vocal.

His first opera, *Die Feen* shelved unheard after acceptance, his second, *Das Liebesverbot* lost after a single performance wherein the singers came to blows and the director decamped without paying salaries, Wagner seized this inauspicious moment to marry an actress, Wilhelmina Planer, and to scrape up enough money by a year's conducting in Russia to go to Paris, where he hoped his luck might turn.

It did,—for the worse. His new opera, *Rienzi*, was so long nobody wanted it. *The Flying Dutchman*, written in seven weeks to beat a competitor, failed of production. *Tannhäuser* and *Lohengrin* shortly afterward met a similar fate. He was reduced to copying music, writing songs, anything to earn a few francs. His exile to Switzerland for radical utterances in 1848 was a disguised blessing, for those quiet years brought forth not alone brilliant essays, but *Tristan und Isolde*, sketches for *Die Meistersinger* and the *Ring Cycle*.

Fresh disaster signalized a second attempt to win the French public. *Tannhäuser* was jeered off the stage, while *Tristan und Isolde* was withdrawn because no soprano could cope with the part. His wife, broken by hardship, left him, but several years later Cosima von Bülow, the daughter of Liszt, divorced her husband to become Frau Wagner. In 1871, a second exile in Switzerland was terminated by a triumphant entry into Baireuth—recognition at last! Here, on a specially constructed stage, he conducted all his operas. *Parsifal*, his last, was completed shortly before his death in 1883.

His romantic tales and the poetic libretti in which he cloaked them, his introduction of bass clarinets and English horns, of divided strings and novel harmonies into the orchestra, his original use of "Leitmotifs" created music-dramas that mark an epoch in the history of the opera. Later composers adopted his mannerisms, but could not match his inspiration, and so he remains, a solitary mountain peak, to which lesser men lift reverent eyes.

Anton Bruckner

"SELF-MADE MUSICIAN"

[Born 1824—Died 1896]

ANTON BRUCKNER was born September 4, 1824, in Ansfelder, near Vienna, but despite his proximity to that great centre of musical activity, he had to create many of his own opportunities for music education. Nevertheless, he became a great organ virtuoso, and, still more important, composer of much lofty music.

His father was a poor village schoolmaster, who could help him with but few advantages. Eventually, however, Anton managed to get lessons with Sechter and Kitzler, and became organist, first at the Institute of St. Florian, then at the Cathedral of Linz. Later he held the position of court organist in Vienna, and professor at the Conservatory there.

His appearance was wholly against him. An awkward peasant, shambling along the street in ill-fitting dusty clothes, with a floppy black hat upon his head and the flowing black tie of a by-gone day, a first-class bore to boot,—it is difficult to discern greatness in such a figure. And during his life-time, there were few who did. It was not until after his death that the efforts of his four friends, Nikisch, Mahler, Hugo Wolf, and Loewe, were rewarded by his recognition, enthusiastic in his own country, slowly growing in others.

The popularity of Brahms, nine years his junior, and his own imitative admiration of Wagner, who preceded him by eleven years, had much to do with this postponement of fame. Moreover, his pieces were unduly long, with such interminable stretches of dreariness between their inspired moments that conductors considerate of their audiences feared to play them. One critic said that he wrote "platitudes under haloes," and that his symphonies were "inlaid with gold and weighted with lead."

Granted that blue-penciling was what his manuscript needed, the fact remains that he has left nine symphonies, three grand *Masses*, a *Te Deum*, and many *Motets*, increasingly liked as they become increasingly familiar. A deep piety brooded over all his writings. When asked if he really believed in God, he replied simply, "How else could I have written the Credo of my *F Minor Mass?*" There is no stress or turbulence, but the ecstasy of the mystic, terrific earnestness,—and—no humor.

He was writing the Ninth Symphony during his last illness, when he was seventy, and his one prayer was that he be allowed to complete it before the end. But the prayer was not granted, for he died leaving but two movements completed, on October 11, 1896.

Max Bruch

"DER HERR PROFESSOR"
[Born 1838—Died 1920]

A BEARDED German who spoke English with a thick accent, who was blunt in his manner, conceited and self-centered, minus charm, grace, or sense of humor, Max Bruch is not a pet with English-speaking biographers, who prefer to dwell upon more ingratiating personalities. Yet his violin concerto in G Minor is ranked among the first five, his choral music is of the finest, and the broad flowing melodies of this composer of the Niederrhein entitle him to a secure position among composers, however biographers may slight him.

He was born in Köln, Germany, on January 6, 1838, and owes much of the inspiration of his early years to his mother, a famous singer. Art beckoned him as alluringly as music, but his study of harmony under Ferdinand Hiller culminated in his winning the Mozart scholarship in Frankfurt at fourteen, and determined his career. He had composed seventy pieces between his ninth and his fourteenth year, when the Köln Philharmonic played his First Symphony.

The rolling-stone life of the musician was his, conducting in Leipsic, where he met Moscheles, Hauptmann and David; in Paris, where Rossini and Berlioz applauded his *Frithjofscenen* Chorus, and in Coblenz. The idea of writing his violin concerto, dedicated to Joachim, came to him while conducting the princely orchestra there. Twelve years later he was summoned to England to conduct, when the great Sarasate played it, and had the satisfaction of hearing it enthusiastically acclaimed, and the gratification of being invited to remain and conduct the Liverpool Philharmonic Orchestra.

He seized the opportunity to perform his own *Odysseus* as well as his setting of Schiller's *Lied von der Glocke*, despite Brahms' slurring comment upon his music: "Yes, I have always thought this *Glocke* of Schiller's one of the greatest *poems* ever written, and I shall continue to hold to that opinion."

But the cry, "Englishmen for English music," was raised against him. Furthermore, his singers rebelled against his exacting training. And so, in 1883, he left England for an American tour, then settled finally in Germany where Prussian and Bavarian orders were pinned upon him, and he was made a Doctor of Music at Cambridge and a member of the Berlin Academy of Arts. The *Scottish Fantasy*, *Romance* for violin and orchestra, and *Achilleus* were his later works. He died in Bonn on September 17, 1920.

Gustav Mahler

Gustav Mahler

"A MODERN WHO BELONGS IN THE PAST"

[*Born 1860—Died 1911*]

LIKE those who wear what fashion does not decree, Gustav Mahler set himself apart from other composers of his day. He refused to consecrate his talents to interpreting the bustle and fret of the contentious modern world he lived in, but attempted, instead, to infuse into his music the classic ideal of the past. This he did at such length that one critic wearily commented, "Mahler was convinced that no symphony could be too long, provided he was the composer."

Born of Jewish parents in Bohemia on July 7, 1860, he followed his general course at the University of Vienna with two years at the Vienna Conservatory under Bruckner. He has been called Bruckner's symphonic successor, as d'Indy was César Franck's, but he was possessed of an austerity and intellectuality which were wholly his own and which had a slightly chastening effect on the music of his day.

One of the great conductors of all time, his life was beset with the difficulties of the lonely, sensitive and irascible soul, who neither understands nor is understood by his fellow-men. Having brought the Vienna Opera to a remarkable degree of perfection, he was obliged to leave that post because of quarrels and intrigues. Tendered the directorship of the Berlin Opera, which had previously declined to engage him because an anti-Semitic trustee "did not like the shape of his nose," he refused, in a haughty telegram, saying, "Cannot accept. Nose still same shape." But the Metropolitan Opera in New York secured him in 1907, and when dissension terminated that engagement, there followed two years with the Philharmonic Orchestra. Even here, his last few concerts were conducted by the first violinist, while Mahler sulked in his hotel over some real or fancied slight. Shortly thereafter he sailed back to Germany, a sick, embittered and disappointed man, there to die May 18, 1911.

A gigantic symphonic work, *Das Lied von der Erde*, and ten lesser symphonies survive him. Number Eight, called the *Symphony of One Thousand* because, in addition to an augmented orchestra, it calls for two mixed choruses, a boys' chorus and eight solo voices, is a remarkable but uneven piece of tonal architecture. Clear rhythm and melody over a most intricate harmonic structure, characterize his work. It is music for the student, not the casual listener. Like the call to prayer, it is unheeded by the many, but reverenced by the few who have ears to hear.

Hugo Wolf

"GENIUS OF MODERN SONG"

[Born 1860—Died 1903]

*I*F EVER a man was "possessed," that man was Hugo Wolf. From the moment of his birth on March 13, 1860, in Vienna, he seemed to be the slave of an inner force wholly beyond his control, which eventually destroyed him, but not before it had driven him to create songs of breathtaking beauty.

Booted from one school to another for failures as a student, he found himself, a very poor young man, compelled to earn his daily bread.

And yet, poor as he was, he proved a most intolerant teacher, who pushed one unfortunate pupil off the piano stool, and spent the hour playing Berlioz for her. When a job as assistant conductor at Salzburg was found to relieve his poverty, he went to claim it weighed down with two bundles,— one large armful containing a plaster cast of Wagner, and one tiny package of socks and shirts, so much less important to him.

A poem that he could love was treasure trove. He would read it aloud so remarkably that all who heard it were spellbound, and then, having steeped himself in it, he would shut himself up, barely eating or sleeping, for months at a time, until the inspiration left him as suddenly as it had come. In this way he wrote in the two years, 1888–90, fifty-three Mörike Lieder, fifty-one Goethe, forty-four Spanish, seventeen Eichendorff, twelve Keller, and a few Italian. After which flood, he wrote despairingly, "I have given up all idea of composing. Pray for my poor soul!" A few more songs the next year, and then for five whole years the muse deserted him completely. But in 1895, he completed the piano score of his opera *Corregidor*, and twenty-two Italian songs. "Auf dem grünen Balkon," "Geh', Geliebte," "Zur Ruh', zur Ruh'," "Der Feuerreiter" are among the best-known of his five hundred songs. They are distinguished for the rare fitness of the music to the spirit and words of the poems, unusual beauty of the piano accompaniments, and extreme breadth, depth, and variety of conception.

Slowly growing recognition, the formation of a Wolfverein to perform his works, the gift of a furnished house and an annuity to relieve his poverty, provided a pleasant lull before the dreadful storm of insanity burst upon him. Again in the clairvoyant mood of composition, he attempted a new opera, *Manuel Venegas*, but he never finished it. After five wretched years in asylums, death released him on February 22, 1903.

Claude Achille Debussy

"THE FIRST MUSICAL IMPRESSIONIST"

[*Born 1862—Died 1918*]

A THIRTY years' war with unfriendly critics culminated in a triumph for Debussy and for his idea of conveying in music the impressions produced by things, rather than the things themselves. But his music betrays no sign of that war. It is purest shimmering melody, based on an unusual scale without semi-tones, a gossamer tissue of strange harmonies so interwoven that it is iridescent, provocative, tantalizingly elusive.

Its writer was that rare phenomenon, a musician who did not leap from his mother's arms to the concert piano. On the contrary, he went normally to school at St. Germain-en-Laye, where he was born September 22, 1862, and grew up with the intention of entering the navy. A musical aunt guided him to the Paris Conservatoire, but he was too impatient of technical drill and too original to excel there either as pianist or composer.

Nevertheless, upon graduation in 1884, his cantata *L'Enfant Prodigue* won him the Prix de Rome, incidentally exiling him from Paris. He was oppressed and unhappy and unable to work in the grandeur of Rome and the close life of the pension for prize-winners. To escape soirées, he concocted a story that he had sold his evening clothes and was too poor to replace them.

When he returned, after the one year's absence which was all he could stand, his orchestral suite *Printemps* brought the critics down upon him. His friends, the poets Verlaine and Baudelaire, and the painters Monet, Pissarro, and Sisley, were kept busy defending him. About fifty songs and seventy-five piano pieces, titled alluringly *Reflets dans l'Eau*, *La Cathedrale Engloutie*, *Les Jardins Sous la Pluie*, etc., sonatas and a string quartette, orchestral works *La Mer* and *L'Aprés-Midi d'un Faune*,—all are stamped with his original quality. His greatest work, the lyric drama *Pelléas et Mélisande*, took ten years to write. It was the first impressionistic opera.

Sensitive and high-strung, he was chronically unhappy. Ugly people and crying children upset him, nevertheless he was wrapt up in the child born in 1904 of his second marriage, "Chou-Chou." To her he dedicated the piano suite *The Children's Corner*, with its charming *Golli-wog's Cake-walk*, *Doll's Serenade*, and *Dr. Gradus ad Parnassum*. She did not long survive him after his death of cancer in 1918.

Vincent d'Indy

"DISCIPLE OF THE GREAT CÉSAR FRANCK"

[*Born 1851—Died 1931*]

SHOULDERS sufficiently broad to carry the mantle of the great César Franck, are to be prized. Vincent d'Indy, one of the Master's favorite pupils, made reverent essayal to continue his tradition after his death, and in so doing, as well as by his own talents, won renown.

Although sophisticated Paris was his birthplace, March 27, 1851, much of his youth was spent at the family estate in the Ardèche region where the spicy scent of the pine woods and the cool Alpine winds became a part of his very being. His mother having died shortly after his birth, his grandmother supervised his education with strong emphasis on its musical side.

Already an accomplished pianist at fourteen, he then turned to the study of harmony, with Lavignac, Diemer and Marmontel. Berlioz' treatise on orchestration, presented by a music-loving uncle, became his Bible, and Berlioz' stormy teachings plus his belief "in Bach, in Beethoven, in Wagner, in good counterpoint, and in God" directed his creative impulse.

The Franco-Prussian War caused a year's interruption of his studies in 1870, but as soon as his uniform was neatly folded away in moth-balls, he presented himself tremblingly to César Franck with a string-quartette he had written. The Master praised its originality, while indicating its weakness, and D'Indy forthwith enrolled as his ardent disciple.

Of his early works, the opera, *Piccolomini*, followed by the oratorio, *Antony and Cleopatra*, are noteworthy, but he achieved his first real success with *Le Chant de la Cloche* (1886), of the Wagnerian school of writing, Leitmotifs, thick harmonies and all. The *Wallenstein Trilogy*, played in 1888, were vigorous, vivid pieces, but the *Istar* symphonic variations, the opera *Fervaal* and the symphonic poem, *Jours d'Été à la Montagne*, represent his best contribution to symphonic writing in France.

As head of the Société Nationale de la Musique and of the Schola Cantorum, in Paris, which he founded, he had his fingers on the musical pulse of the world. The clinical histories of many new compositions appeared in current periodicals in brilliant articles from his pen, and he also found time to write biographies of César Franck and Beethoven.

When he died of heart failure, December 3, 1931, honorary societies the world over mourned the loss of a cherished member, distinguished for dignity, sincerity, industry and inspiration.

Paul Abraham Dukas

"FRENCH CLASSICIST AMONG THE MODERNS"

[*Born October 1, 1865—*   ]

T HERE is an amusing legend of a sorcerer's apprentice, who, having decided to play the magician in his master's absence, commanded the broom to carry in a pail of water. He forgot the magic words that would check its activity, and broke it in half, when to his horror, both halves became water-carriers. A flood was barely averted by the opportune return of the sorcerer.

Paul Dukas has earned the everlasting gratitude of concert-goers, old and young, by his humorous orchestral version of this story, *L'Apprenti Sorcier*, which has leavened many a dreary symphonic program with its rhythmically comic strains. It is strange that humor should be our first thought in connection with Dukas, for he is a serious, scholarly, meditative soul, described by a friend as "un solitaire de l'espèce souriante."

He was born in Paris on October 1, 1865, and distinguished himself upon graduation from the Conservatoire by winning, not the first, but the second Prix de Rome, therein departing from the example set by most of the illustrious composers. Instead of returning for a fresh attempt at it, he withdrew for a long period of study and research, literary and philosophical, as well as musical. When he re-entered active life, it was as teacher, composer, and writer of high attainments.

The fruits of his study have appeared in the form of numerous thoughtful articles in periodicals, and in transcriptions of compositions which he admired, especially those of Rameau, Cherubini, Saint-Saëns, and Wagner. His *Variations on a Theme of Rameau*, for piano, are the best of these.

Outstanding among his original compositions are *Ariane et Barbe Bleue*, the operatic woes of Bluebeard and his seven wives, produced in 1907 at the Opéra Comique in Paris, and later at the Metropolitan Opera in New York, and ranked by critics beside Debussy's *Pelléas et Mélisande;* three orchestral overtures; a ballet, *Le Péri;* the Symphony in C Major, containing as scherzo *L'Apprenti Sorcier;* and the *Piano Sonata* dedicated to Saint-Saëns.

In his style there is a combination of classicism with romanticism. The highly expressive subjects of his choice receive freely imaginative treatment, but such adherence to form as might be expected of a scholar. A great admirer of Wagner, he abhors schools of writing, and has frequently quoted to his own students Wagner's precept. "Ne soyez d'aucune école, surtout pas de la mienne."

Maurice Ravel

"LEADER OF THE MODERN FRENCH SCHOOL"

[*Born March 7, 1875—*   ]

A WISE little bird, head cocked and bright eye unwinking, surveying the entire field of music, with intent to build his own musical nest upon the location most pleasing to him, is Ravel. A close kinship with the spontaneous melodies of Mozart does not deter him from following the impressionistic lead of Debussy, the romanticism of Chabrier, the humor of Satie, the clear precision of Fauré. But the originality with which he creates modern music upon classic forms frees him from any possible charge of imitation. "In art," he once said, "nothing is left to chance." And this is true of his own art, his own life.

Born on March 7, 1875, in Cibourc in the Basse-Pyrenées, educated in Paris and at the Conservatoire, he won the second Prix de Rome in 1901, and in the course of the same year produced a piano piece, *Jeux d'Eaux*, so original in style and content that it won immediate praise. The beautiful *String Quartette in F*, *Scheherezade*, written for three voices and orchestra, *Les Miroirs*, *Valses Nobles et Sentimentales*, and such well-known piano pieces as *Pavane pour un Enfant Defunte*, *Gaspard de la Nuit*, appeared before 1914.

Summoned to military duty by the World War, he undertook to drive a motor-truck, and within a year this gay musician who resembled an American college boy, became a tense, high-strung man with gray-streaked hair. His delicate health proved quite unequal to this rough task, and in 1915 an honorable discharge enabled him to return to his work.

For two years he went into retirement with a piano concerto, over which he labored from ten to twelve hours daily, achieving a triumph when he gave it to the world. The *Trio;* the orchestral suites *Daphnis et Chloe*, *Ma Mère l'Oye*, *Le Tombeau de Couperin*, *Rhapsodie Espagnole;* the ballet *L'Enfant et les Sortilèges;* and the throbbing *Bolero* which Toscanini introduced to America, have added many cubits to his musical stature. Clear, logical, well-proportioned and well-balanced, with an exquisite sense of effect, they are characteristic of the man and his art.

In his retreat at Montfort-L'Amaury, near Versailles, where a housekeeper, many paintings and six Siamese cats bear him company, this polished, witty aristocrat renounces the world, except for occasional travels. He has been to Vienna and London, has toured the United States, and is not in the least provincial, but he is happiest working in his own way, under his own vine and fig-tree.

Edward Elgar

Sir Edward Elgar

"ENGLAND'S MUSICIAN LAUREATE"

[Born 1857—   ]

W HEN Edward Elgar was born near Worcester, England, June 2, 1857, his father was both organist of the Roman Catholic Church of St. George's and owner of a music warehouse. The boy thus learned to play the gamut of musical instruments from organ to deep bassoon, and when he succeeded his father as organist, his orchestrations were the richer for this rare opportunity.

Possessed of a deeply religious nature, his genius found its highest expression in church music, though to the popular mind he is best known for his *Pomp and Circumstance*, written that soldiers might march the better at the coronation of Edward VII, and played ever since to accompany college graduates on their exit into the wide world.

For his *Dream of Gerontius*, with its twelve-part chorus, based upon Cardinal Newman's poem, Ernest Newman, eminent British critic, claims that it is "one of the most remarkable achievements in *all* music and one that cannot die so long as men's souls are vexed by the problems of life and death," while his *A Flat Symphony* and his *Enigma Variations* transfigure the soul's strivings into music of rare beauty. In his writing he escaped from tradition and created a language better fitted to express his preoccupation with the spiritual.

Knighted in 1904, when the Elgar Festival filled Covent Garden for a three-day program; granted the Order of Merit by the Royal Philharmonic Society in 1926; asked to conduct a program of his own works in Queen's Hall in 1930, he has been the recipient of many honors in his own day and from his own countrymen. With a "laugh like a minor second which is never resolved," conversation "presto scherzando," and one of the most gracious ladies of England for a wife, he has had all the elements that make for popularity.

While Professor of Music at Birmingham University, he asserted himself as champion of absolute music, declaring program music to be mere literature, and only that to be real music which gives no clue to its meaning. But in the defense of this thesis he was not as effective as in his championing of "musical education which shall tend to create listeners, not merely executants." In the gramophone and later the radio, he saw boundless opportunity for bringing "the best music to the people least able to pay for it," and has lived to hear his own compositions come back to him through the ether from every country in Europe and across the vast Atlantic.

Albéniz

Isaac Albeniz

"THE WILD MAN FROM SPAIN"

[Born 1860—Died 1909]

*I*N HIS youth a mad scapegrace, in middle age so fat he could hardly sit comfortably at the piano, Isaac Albeniz presents a life full of fascinating contrasts.

He was born in Camprodon, Spain, on May 29, 1860, one of five children,—the most troublesome, as the most talented one. Two years after he had appeared at Barcelona, aged four, as an infant prodigy, he presented himself for examination at the Conservatoire in Paris. While his judges were marveling at his performance, he rose from the piano stool, drew a hard rubber ball from his pocket and threw it at the mirror in the room, shattering it,—just for fun. He was not admitted!

Running away from home was his pet pastime. After wandering about Spain playing in cafés and hobnobbing with bandits, he stowed away on a boat to South America when he was eleven, and by the time he landed, he had paid his way and had a sheaf of letters of introduction from passengers to boot.

His father happened to hear his performance in a Havana café, and induced him with the promise of lessons to come home. From then on, he never stopped studying, the list of his teachers reads like a musical "Who's Who,"—Jadassohn, Reinecke, DuPont, Gevaert, Liszt, and many more.

The copyright of his swinging *Pavana* was sold for the price of a bull-fight ticket, and he had to tour constantly to pay the expenses his generosity was always incurring. When he was made conductor of the Prince of Wales Theatre in London, the need for money kept him composing at the theatre during rehearsals, a copyist catching the sheets as they fell from his hands.

But Paris and such men as Debussy, Fauré, Chausson, and D'Indy beckoned in the early '90s, so he settled down there with his wife and three children and his good friend Arbos near by, to gain weight, to play the piano, and to compose his most important works.

Iberia, his best-known piano suite, written while he, his wife, and his daughter were all ill in Nice, is filled with the conflicting rhythms, the wavering melodies, the strong colors of Spain; *Catalonia*, written shortly after, hardly less so. It is a great pity that just as he had mastered his art and was producing truly important work, death should have claimed him June 16, 1909, at the age of forty-nine. It may be said that his death marked the end of the first period of the Spanish musical Renaissance.

Enrique Granados y Campina
"INTERPRETER OF SPAIN IN SONG AND DANCE"
[Born 1867—Died 1916]

THE plaster walls of his study were hung with paintings by Velasquez and Goya; two pianos faced each other amiably from opposite corners of the room; antique chairs creaked under friendly visitors. Against this background, Granados, his adored wife, and any of the six children who happened to be about, dispensed memorable hospitality.

He was a Catalonian, born in Lerida July 29, 1867. Owing to delicate health, his early studies were somewhat irregular, and he was unable to complete his course at the Conservatoire in Paris, but worked privately instead with De Beriot. His compositions, consequently, are more praised for their originality than for their perfection of form. The expression of feeling was, to his mind, the primary purpose of music, and he wrote with that ideal constantly in mind.

Endowed with the passionate languor of his race, sensitive, intuitive, he was described as "one of the most delicious visionaries among the artists." Not the castanet-clicking, bull-fighting Spain of the foreigner, but the tragic, primitive peasant land he knew lives in his writing. In the *Tonadillas*, *Spanish Dances* and the opera, *Goyescas*, he succeeded so well that Casals said to him, "Granados, every form you employ has been employed before, and yet from them you have evolved something never heard in the world before."

There are many works, *Maria del Carmen*, an opera; *Miel d'Alcaria* and *Dante;* piano suite, *Elisande; Canciones Amatores; Valses Poetiques;* some chamber music. When he played his own piano pieces, he could convince any critic of their greatness, so brilliant was his execution.

The opera, *Goyescas*, the first Spanish opera to be produced at the Metropolitan in New York, was his swan song and his sweetest. Suggested by the brilliant paintings of Goya, it is a story of love, of jealousy and revenge. The composer himself brought it to America and witnessed its triumph with such satisfaction as should reward the man who has for twenty years endured the drudgery of teaching rather than commercialize his art by writing unworthily.

As fate would have it, he embarked on the English boat, *Sussex*, on his return trip. She was torpedoed by a German submarine March 24, 1916. Granados escaped to a life-boat, but seeing his wife struggling in the waves, jumped overboard to rescue her. They were drowned together, romantically clasped in each other's arms.

Manuel de Falla y Mateu

"A POST-VICTORIAN SPANIARD"

[Born November 23, 1876—   ]

*I*N GRANADOS, at the foot of the snow-capped Sierra Nevadas, with the sound of church bells and rushing waters creating a perpetual music about him, lives Manuel de Falla, son of Spain, and one of her great musical exponents.

His dreamy melancholy nature may have been an inheritance from the mother who gave birth to him in Cadiz on November 23, 1876. Like a shy wraith, shrinking from reality, he has traversed the years, living up to the inscriptions on a vase presented by some friends: "I am the palpable ghost of Don Manuel de Falla y Mateu."

Perhaps his years of obscure poverty in Paris from 1907 to 1914 intensified that shyness. He himself tells the story of how he presented himself, when he was almost starving, at the home of a wealthy prospective pupil who had been recommended to him, and being received as a delinquent tradesman on account of the brown paper parcel of his laundry he was carrying, was too abashed to explain who he was, despite his great need, and was ignominiously shown the door. But he made friends in Paris— Debussy, Dukas and Charpentier all recognized his talent and influenced it in one way or another, if only by sending him home more Spanish than ever.

Endeavoring always to surpass himself, he has not produced a great mass of work, but has labored painstakingly over his slender output. Albeniz' ideal of stressing the emotional individuality of his country rather than its picturesqueness has also been his.

Operas, *La Vida Breve* and *Il Retablo de Maese Pedro*, the latter played with marionettes; ballets, *The Three-Cornered Hat* and *Love the Magician; Pièces Espagnoles* and *Fantaisie Boetica* for piano, including the famous *Danse Rituelle de Feu; Three Melodies for Violin and Piano;* a splendid *Concerto for Cembalo* have been played, most of them at the De Falla festival in Barcelona in 1926.

Mme. Wanda Landowska, to whom the concerto is dedicated, played with all the more fervor on this occasion as she had been its original inspiration. When she had visited De Falla in Granados some years previously, he was as pleased with the harpsichord under her magic fingers as with a new toy and vowed then to write a piece worthy of such a performer.

More rhythmical than melodious, more expressive than picturesque or descriptive, enlivened with original tunes so characteristic that they sound like genuine folk-melodies, his music is powerful, yet popular. He stands as the connecting link between ultra-modern Spanish music and the conventional strains of the bland Victorian era.

Jan Sibelius

"SOLITARY FINNISH GENIUS"

[*Born December 8, 1865—*   ]

SIBELIUS remarked of himself a few years ago that whereas other composers were busy mixing musical cocktails, he offered the public nothing but a drink of pure cold water. But a people surfeited with alcohol turns gratefully to the refreshment of water, and so it is that his fame, always considerable in his own country, has extended until to-day he is recognized, as not alone a great Finnish composer, but one of the great composers of the world.

An uneventful life, free of struggle, has enabled him to work without hindrance. Born of a music-loving family of doctors and lawyers in Tavastehus, Finland (December 8, 1865), he followed the study of law despite a strange propensity for roaming the woods with his violin under his arm, dreaming and improvising as he went. But he finally put the law behind him, and studied music at the Conservatory of Helsingfors under Wegelius, later spending a few years in Berlin and Vienna. When he returned to Helsingfors, it was to become director of the Conservatory, to receive a comfortable annuity from the state, to marry Aino Jarnefelt, herself an artist and musician, and to settle down to the creative work made possible by such a happy combination of circumstances.

His earlier compositions, *The Swan of Tuonela*, *Lennikainen*, and *En Saga*, all orchestral, won him the unchallenged name of interpreter of the soul of his country. He used no folk-songs, but created his own so tellingly that the hills and streams and woodlands of Finland, and the runes of the national *Kalevala* pertaining thereto are recreated for the listener.

The eight symphonies of his maturer days, after 1899, while still national, are more tranquil, more philosophic, more in the nature of absolute music. *Symphony Number IV*, a cry of desolation and despair, has the innate gravity and restrained melancholy of the Finnish temperament, never breaking into uncontrolled sobs as does Tchaikowsky's *Pathetique*, for example. His violin concerto, string quartette, and such orchestral pieces as *Finlandia*, *Valse Triste* and *King Christian II*, display his strongly individual mode of expression. While conforming to the rules of harmony and form, he has his own peculiar message and his own peculiar way of conveying it. Natural, direct thinking, magnificent economy in writing and classic purity of thought coupled with the full resources of the orchestra are some of the earmarks of his genius.

Since the national celebration of his sixtieth birthday, he has lived in his villa, Tarvenpaa, near Helsingfors, respected and honored by the entire world.

Arnold Schoenberg

"GENIUS OR MADMAN?"

[Born September 13, 1874—   ]

ARNOLD SCHOENBERG's music has never left an audience unmoved. Of it James Huneker commented bitterly: "If such music-making is ever to become accepted, then I long for Death, the Releaser." At the first performance of the *Five Pieces for Orchestra* in Paris, 1923, Schoenberg's friend and fellow-composer, Florent Schmitt, was deprived of voice and eye-glasses, shouting in his defense. One humorist rose after hearing the *First String Quartette* and whistled a derisive solo on his latchkey as he made his exit.

The man behind this music appears, in person, to be anything but a sensation-monger. So gifted that he could teach himself enough violin and cello to take part in chamber-music throughout his school life in Vienna, able to compose with only his own study of the great masters to guide him, and a few lessons from his brother-in-law at twenty, he won his positions as professor of harmony at various conservatories purely on the strength of his much-decried compositions.

His life as a composer falls into three periods. During the first, when Beethoven, Bach and Mozart were his models, his sextet, *Die Verklärte Nacht*, a "sort of *Tristan and Isolde* on the strings," and his quartette, "a sad negation of all that is artistic," were his outstanding contributions. They are simplicity itself, compared with the *Gurrelieder* of his second period. This Gargantuan work, written for five solo voices, a reciter, two choruses and an orchestra of 114, is music for hardened listeners. Special manuscript paper of forty-eight lines was required to write down its complicated orchestration. The symphonic poem, *Pelléas et Melisande*, the *Kammersinfonie*, *Second String Quartette*, *Six Songs for Orchestra*, all of the second period, reach, by means of a most complex polyphonic structure, toward new realms of tone, a new freedom of expression.

The work of his mature years comprises the *Georglieder*, *Pierre Lunaire*, *Erwartung*, *Die Glückliche Hand* and smaller pieces. They are characterized by the absence of fixed tonality, by chords based on intervals of fourths instead of the usual thirds, by absolutely free rhythms and by revolutionary instrumentation of every sort. No wonder it takes time to grow accustomed to such strange sounds.

Yet there is an increasing group of disciples who accept his dictum that "The artist does, not what *others* consider beautiful, but what, for him, is a necessity" and that "the main thing is to seek." Like Mussolini, he has such a compelling magnetism that those who come to scoff at his music frequently remain to pray.

Ernest Bloch

"EXPONENT OF RACIAL MUSIC"

[*Born July 24, 1880—*   ]

THE fact that Ernest Bloch is a Swiss, born in Geneva on July 24, 1880, has not resulted in his producing essentially Swiss music, any more than his selling cuckoo-clocks for awhile to earn a living made a clock-maker of him. But the fact that he is a Jew, with a deep love of Old Testament sonorities, has given to his compositions an unique racial savor which sets them apart from other modern compositions. He himself made the statement, "Nationalism is not essential in Music; race consciousness is."

He is a vibrant dramatic mystic. His training was excellent,—rhythm with Dalcroze, violin with Ysaye, counterpoint with Hesse and Knorr, the latter of whom, he said, taught him the greatest thing of all,—to teach himself. And on the strength of that, he taught others also, at Geneva Conservatory, at the Mannes School in New York, at Cleveland Conservatory for five years, and at the San Francisco Conservatory.

His coming to America was accomplished under somewhat discouraging conditions. He left Geneva to lead an orchestra on tour with Maud Allan, the dancer, and found himself stranded in New York in 1915, when the company went bankrupt. A year in obscurity in a furnished room ensued, from which Karl Muck summoned him to Boston to conduct his *Trois Poèmes Juifs* with the Boston Symphony Orchestra, and from then on his qualities as a composer have been generally recognized.

Schelomo, a rhapsody for cello and orchestra, is the Song of Solomon translated into deeply expressive music; it carries Solomon in all his glory into the realms of sound, with a wealth of harmonic invention and majestic melodic line. *America,* the epic orchestral rhapsody which won the $3000 prize offered by *Musical America* in 1926, bears as its dedication, "Oh America, because you build for mankind, I build for you." It culminates in a stirring anthem which he hopes may supplant the English drinking song now in common use as the national anthem.

Sincerity is the key-note of the man and his works. A composer must write as he feels, for what he is will appear in his music, even his insincerity, according to Bloch's belief. And in his *Symphony in C minor,* his *Symphony Israel* (on Hebrew themes), *String-Quartette in B,* and *Viola-Suite,* he writes consistently with this philosophy.

Sergei Vassilievitch Rachmaninoff

"MELANCHOLY HIGH-PRIEST OF RUSSIAN MUSIC"

[*Born April 1, 1873—*]

THE virtuoso Rachmaninoff of the concert stage broods darkly over his key-board, deliberately prolonging that pregnant moment before releasing the pent-up power of his art. The composer Rachmaninoff is equally deliberate. Not for him the easy flow of instinctive creation,— his is a slow, painful concentrated process, which absorbs him from nine in the morning until eleven at night, permitting no interruption or other form of occupation. When composing, he is all composer; when playing, all pianist; when conducting, all conductor; and in all three fields he is a genius.

Revolutions have shattered his scheme of life. Brought up on the family estate Oneig in Novgorod, where he was born on April 1, 1873, he inherited the tradition of an aristocratic grandfather who was at the same time a remarkable pianist. When a revolution in the family fortunes sent him at nine to the Conservatory instead of to an expensive noblemen's school, he absorbed thirstily the piano instruction of Zvereff and Siloti, the theory of Taneyev and Arensky. His opera *Aleko* won him a gold medal at graduation, but the *Trio Élegiaque* and *First Symphony*, in which he followed his adored Tschaikowsky too closely for his own good, were not well received.

For three years he wrote nothing in consequence, taking refuge from his failure in a life of Bohemian irregularity. To the doctor who hypnotized him back to normal living he dedicated his second and perhaps finest piano concerto in 1901. His piano works include four concertos, two suites, five pieces including the famous C # Minor Prelude, and others. The *Second Symphony* and famous symphonic poem *The Isle of the Dead* are outstanding orchestral works, while two operas, and a song cycle dedicated to Nina Koshetz appeared before the Russian Revolution drove him, in 1918, to retrieve his financial fortunes by concertizing, first in Europe, then in America, where he proceeded to make his home.

A deep-seated sadness, almost melancholy, settled upon this "man without a country," and inspiration deserted him so completely that only his *Fourth Piano Concerto* and three songs have broken an eight years' silence. But his past compositions, imbued with the enigmatic quality of a deeply thoughtful and truly great spirit and characterized by lyric themes, dark sonorities in the orchestra, rich romantic harmonies, have won him a place somewhere between romantic tradition and ultra-modern ideals as a strongly-forged and indispensable connecting link.

Igor Stravinsky

"RUSSIAN ARBITER OF MUSICAL FASHION"

[*Born June 17, 1882*—   ]

THE life of Igor Stravinsky, from his birth in Petrograd on June 17, 1882, was a series of daring musical experiments. His father, Feodor, an opera-singer, fed him law instead of the music that was to be expected, but when, at twenty, the young man met Rimsky-Korsakov while traveling in Europe, he impulsively bade farewell to legal study and attached himself to that composer as pupil and friend.

In January, 1906, he took two momentous steps,—he married, and he decided to become a composer. With the instinct for fashion of a born Beau Brummel, he noted that Russian opera was out of favor, and Russian ballet, thanks to Diaghileff, very much in. So he exploded two ballets, *The Firebird*, and *Fireworks*, in Paris with such a loud bang that his name resounded from the din as a composer to be reckoned with. Other ballets,— *Petroushka* (perhaps his masterpiece), *The Nightingale*, *The Rite of Spring*, are justly popular. The barbaric rhythms of the last caused women to faint with excitement at its first performance. A combination of exquisiteness with terrific power, of gorgeous picturesqueness with a tang of humor, they set a new musical fashion, being neither stereotyped on the one hand nor ear-shattering on the other.

But wearying of grandiose researches into orchestra and ballet he turned his nimble talent to smaller forms and ensembles, with an appreciative eye upon the classics. In *Pulcinella*, a charming arrangement of the Pergolesi ballet; *Renard*, and *Mavra*, comic operas; a string quartette; and piano pieces for children, he squeezed tubes of gorgeous color on miniature palettes, evoking new sounds from the same old instruments and the same old diatonic scales. His piano concerto and sonata were an experiment in "fake Bach," not entirely a happy one, while an étude written especially for the player-piano permitted him to dabble in mechanics

He gave a new twist to the musical mode with *Oedipus Rex*, a gigantic oratorio sung in Latin with full orchestra. This work, the ballet *Apollon Musagete*, and the violin concerto have disappointed many admirers of his earlier style. They find themselves unable to discern the old Stravinsky in the new, no longer strongly Russian, strongly exotic, strongly realistic, strongly anything. Nevertheless they continue to hope for novelty from the slight, dynamic little man, monocle in shrewd eye, described as a "kind of musical bank director." He has achieved a firm footing in the western world, where he has traveled and conducted extensively, as a composer of true, sometimes beautiful music expressive of the twentieth century.

Sergei Prokofiev

"STRONG MAN OF REVOLUTIONARY RUSSIA"

[*Born April 23, 1891—*   ]

A TRICKSY sprite, bubbling over musically with mischief and puck-ishness was young Prokofiev, born in Moscow, April 23, 1891. The fact that he wrote his first piece at five, three operas by the time he was thirteen, and over one hundred pieces during his years at the Petrograd Conservatory (1904–9), may explain the extreme freshness of his early works. All his youth was spontaneously poured into them, and, like Peter Pan, he showed no sign of losing that youth in the process of growing up.

He followed his First Piano Concerto, which won the Rubinstein prize when he was graduated, with a second and a third; with a gay ballet, *Chout*, about a couple of buffoons and their humorous haps and mishaps; with the *Sarcasmes;* with a suite *Scythia* (also called *Ala and Lolli*), whose fearless harmonies drove the composer Glazounov from the hall where it was being performed. He marked almost everything "féroce,"—there was a boldness, a rough contempt for mere prettiness, a vivid picturesqueness in these early works which won them loud huzzas in Russia.

The green powers which produced such musical colic in Glazounov ripened considerably after Prokofiev left Russia to make a concert tour (1918). Having elected to travel to America via Siberia and the Mongolian desert, he arrived with his new opera, *The Love for Three Oranges*, whose nonsense heaped on nonsense brought grand opera down to earth with a stimulating shock.

His ballet *The Prodigal Son* might almost be said to have marked the return of this musical prodigal to the fatted calf of lyrical beauty after a debauch of wit and humor. From now on, he stood for simplification, conciseness, less emotion; for sharp melodic line and concise rhythm; for design rather than color. He married in 1921, and visited the United States frequently thereafter, constantly adding new compositions. A quartette for four bassoons; a quintette for oboe, clarinet, violin, viola and double bass; and finally the ballet, *Pas d'Acier* (Age of Steel), which glorifies machinery in rocking rhythmic dissonances, are his latest attempts to interpret the age he lives in.

This Revolutionary who looks like a clear-eyed boy has done his best to mask with humor the curiously tender spirit which peeps through his grinning mask despite his shamefaced attempts to hide it. In expressing his musical ideas, he has been wholly fearless, wholly himself, wholly modern, and so has earned the title of founder of a new Russian school, first of a new musical era.

Ottorino Respighi

"A MODERN ITALIAN TURNS TO CLASSIC GREECE"

[Born July 9 1879—   ]

ON THE highest of the seven hills of Rome, overlooking that eternal city, perches the villa of Ottorino Respighi. His appreciation of the architectural splendors of a bygone day seems to have colored his feeling toward the music of that day, for here is one modern who has surveyed the field of music and gone to the Greek modes for inspiration. He has, moreover, stated that music which is simple is interesting, and that dissonance for its own sake is abhorrent to him, although as a means of expression it has important uses.—neither of which may be described as tenets of ultramodern thought

Born in Bologna, July 9, 1879, his father Giuseppe, a pianist, his grand-father choir-master in the church, there was no lack of music in his home. His father prepared him to enter the Liceo Musicale in Bologna, where he studied under Sarti, Torchi, and Martinucci, and carried off prizes for violin and composition. Max Bruch in Berlin and Rimsky-Korsakov in Petrograd gave him an admixture of German and Russian technic, and made a linguist of him besides, so that he was fully qualified for the position of Professor of Harmony at the Liceo S. Cecilia in Rome, a position which he resigned in 1926 to devote himself wholly to composition.

He has produced a greater number and variety of works than any twentieth century Italian, even Casella, representative of the extremist school. His operas are *Rè Enzo*, *Semirâma*, *Maria Vittoria*, and *Belfagor*, with a puppet play, *The Sleeping Princess*. The symphonic poems—*Pines of Rome*, *Fountains of Rome*, and *Festivals of Rome*, the first with its novel intro-duction of the song of the nightingale in a gramophone record, have been played in America with great success. In the *Gregorian Concerto* for violin and the *Mixolydian* for piano he revived the religious sobriety of medieval-ism for the modern audience. There are ballets, *Venetian Scherzo*, *La Boutique Fantasque*, etc., chamber music, a *Toccata* for piano and orchestra, a cantata, *Primavera*, numerous suites, such as *The Birds*, *Church-Windows*, *Suites for Lute*, arrangements and transcriptions galore. His orchestral works have re-awakened interest in the symphony in song-loving Italy.

When his miracle play, *Maria Egeziaca*, was produced in New York in 1932, the composer, "beaming and Beethovenish of countenance," was present with his wife, the singer Elsa Ollivieri, to acknowledge the plaudits of the audience. A thing of profound sincerity, vibrant with feeling, its appeal is for those who listen to music simply, reverently, believingly, with faith as did the medieval listeners.

Edward MacDowell

Edward MacDowell

"CELTIC POET IN AMERICAN MUSIC"

[Born 1861—Died 1908]

AN OVERWHELMINGLY creative person, this Edward MacDowell, who planned gardens, designed buildings, decorated rooms, photographed, and painted pictures, besides playing the piano like an angel and composing music that placed him high in the ranks of American composers.

His talent was fostered from the moment of his birth in New York December 18, 1861. Local teachers did fairly well by him, Carreno encouraged him, and at fifteen his mother took him abroad. He studied at the Paris and Frankfurt Conservatories, learning much from Raff, taught in Darmstadt, then settled in Wiesbaden. Marian Nevins, a student whom he hesitated to accept as a piano-pupil on the ground that American girls never worked seriously, took her revenge by marrying him in 1884. Four years later they returned together to America, living first in Boston, then in New York.

The "rotten melodies," as he called them, which his wife often fished from the scrap-basket after he had crumpled them in disgust, are for the most part based on definite poetic images, subtly incorporated with personal feeling. He loved poetry. His early creative life was really a preparation for the major works of his later years,—the *Woodland Sketches*, *Fireside Tales*, *Sea Pieces*, *New England Idylls*, *Norse* and *Keltic Sonatas*, the *Indian Suite*, and such songs and piano pieces as *To a Wild Rose*, *The West Wind Croons in the Cedar Tree*, *Moonshine*. It is his piano pieces which are oftenest played to-day.

The music department of Columbia University, of which he assumed the chair in 1896, owed much to the teaching of this handsome exuberant genius, whose courses in history and appreciation of music gave undergraduates a live interest in what had hitherto been a dead subject. But eight years of this work, rendered doubly difficult by the opposition of conservative authorities to his "advanced ideas," proved too much.

In 1904, his mind gave way, and Mrs. MacDowell led him, gentle and docile, to the home in Peterboro where they had spent many happy summers. He became as a child, thumbing the pages of fairy-tales he could not read, and so died peacefully on January 23, 1908. But young creative artists rise up and call him blessed, for the house in Peterboro, with Mrs. MacDowell as its presiding genius, is thrown open to them in the summer, just as its owner's radiant personality was thrown open to them during the summer of his life.

Deems Taylor

"PRACTICAL MAN OF DREAMS"

[*Born December 22, 1885—*]

*I*T's much more uncomfortable not writing music when you want to, than writing it," was Deems Taylor's explanation of the reason why the diverse roads he has traveled have all led him to the Rome of his heart's desire.

Alert, highly geared, modern in the best sense, he is a typical product of New York, where he was born and educated. He went to New York University, and as he planned to become an architect his course was conspicuously free from such irrelevant matter as music. Nevertheless he wrote musical comedies, four in four years, although ten months' piano instruction and six summer-school weeks of harmony and counterpoint were all the equipment he could add to his talent.

Jobs with encyclopedias, trade journals, magazines; jobs as war correspondent, lecturer, commercial artist, editor, theatre pianist, provided him with three meals daily, and with his blue and white country retreat in Connecticut, and left him a minimum of leisure for study and composition.

His first musical comedy success, *The Echo* died after six months. So, having read of a prize to be given by the National Federation of Music Clubs for a symphonic poem, he decided to "go high-brow" and won it with *Siren Song*. *The Chambered Nautilus*, written in 1916, and *The Looking-Glass Suite*, two years later, won him his first public recognition.

In 1921 he married Mary Kennedy, the actress, and secured the job of music critic on the *New York World* also, and for four years his brilliant comment was the salt on the breakfast-egg of every music-lover in New York. His incidental music to *Liliom* and *Beggar on Horseback* again won him so much glory, that when, in 1925, the Metropolitan Opera management asked him to suggest an American composer to write an opera, his retort, "Why not commission me?" was accepted in all seriousness.

The King's Henchman, libretto by Edna St. Vincent Millay, was the first outcome of this conference, *Peter Ibbetson*, in 1929, the second. Sung in English, they are the first attempt to create "English-speaking music," wherein the line of the music follows the natural inflections of the voice speaking not German or Italian, but English. The triple union of song, words, and orchestra, thus achieved, resolves the traditional conflict among the three.

Even as he has balanced voice with orchestra in opera, so has he balanced dream with reality in his life, and won through to deserved success in both.

John Alden Carpenter

"ALL-AMERICAN COMPOSER"

[*Born February 28, 1876—*   ]

A COMPOSER who makes a good living as a business man is usually considered not in a class with one who starves at it. That John Alden Carpenter has been called by one critic the logical successor to MacDowell should prove that he has lived down his affluence—perhaps has even had it accepted as an extra manifestation of his Americanism.

Born in Park Ridge, Illinois, February 28, 1876, he had his first lessons from his mother, a talented singer. Later, when he went to Harvard, he devoured all the music courses in the catalogue, wrote the music for the Hasty-Pudding Club and was President of the Glee Club. He studied first with Elgar in London, later with Ziehn in Chicago, where he made his home and his living as vice-president of George B. Carpenter and Co., mill supplies.

In 1914 his orchestral suite, *Adventures in a Perambulator*, an impressionistic picture of an infant's mental processes, witty, tuneful and distinctively American, won him amused recognition. A year later came his charming *Concertino for Piano and Orchestra*, which he described as a "light-hearted conversation between piano and orchestra." *A Symphony*, *The Pilgrim Vision* and *Jazz Pieces*, all for orchestra, followed.

It was in ballet that this quiet gentleman best voiced the spirit of America. *The Birthday of the Infanta*, a first attempt, preceded the successful *Krazy Kat* in 1921, based on the Herriman newspaper cartoons. *Skyscrapers* was that anomaly, a ballet where the music was written before the libretto. Six months' retirement in a Vermont farmhouse with Robert Edmond Jones, Carpenter playing his score over and over, suggested to Jones the mobile stage settings and the posturings of the dance which the Metropolitan Opera used in its 1926 production. A noisy, fantastic picture of the alternation of work and play in American life, it represents an attempt to capture the spirit of jazz and fix it in orchestral sonority.

His songs, *Gitanjali*, to the text of Tagore, and *Water-Colors*, based on four Chinese poems, present another popular aspect of his art. Warm, sensitive, full of color, elegance and refinement, they are wholly successful in their genre, although the *Improving Songs for Anxious Children* are more widely sung. *The Song of Faith*, completed in 1932 for the Washington Bicentennial, was described by Lawrence Gilman as "no mere patriotic ballyhoo and jingoistic eagle-shrieking" but as "music of faith and love and elevation." The same words, perhaps, may be used to define this composer's quality at its best.

Samuel Coleridge-Taylor

"THE BLACK MAN WHO INTERPRETS HIS RACE"

[Born 1875—Died 1912]

WHEN Samuel Coleridge-Taylor's black father deserted his white mother shortly after Samuel's birth in London on August 15, 1875, friends came to their aid, as friends always did throughout the short thirty-seven years of his life. Joseph Beckwith, conductor of a theatre orchestra in Croydon, saw the handsome little seven-year-old mulatto playing marbles in the street one day, with a small violin tucked under his arm. Much intrigued, he invited the boy in, and having heard him play, gave him violin-lessons free for the next seven years. A certain Colonel Walters, who heard his clear treble voice above the others in his school chorus, practically became his guardian, placing him in a choir, and at fifteen sending him to the Royal College of Music, where he studied composition as well as violin.

While teaching, after graduation, at the Croydon Conservatory of Music, Samuel conducted the string orchestra there, and "the little dark man with the big white stick" became very popular. His romance with Jessie Walmisley, a fellow student, culminated in their marriage, despite her family's opposition to the mixture of races.

Anthems, chamber-music, *Southern Love-Songs*, and *African Romances* for violin had already made him known as composer. In 1901 his cantata, *Hiawatha's Wedding-feast*, with its tender love-song, "Onaway, awake, beloved" achieved phenomenal success. *The Hiawatha Overture, Death of Minnehaha* and *Hiawatha's Departure* completed a magnificent cycle. His second child was named Hiawatha after his musical hero.

His tour of America in 1904 increased his popularity, likewise his determination to further the interests of his race. His music was distinctly racial, with strong, clear-cut rhythms, abundant melody, solid chords, vivid contrasts, and climaxes comparable to the negro spirituals. In his *African Suite*, the symphonic poem *Toussaint l'Ouverture* and his settings of the poems of his friend Paul Dunbar, the negro poet, he tried to do for negro music what Brahms did for Hungarian, Dvořák for Bohemian, Grieg for Norwegian music.

Sensitive, kindly, utterly simple and lovable, he was only thirty-seven, and had just completed his suite, *Tale of Old Japan*, and a violin concerto, when he contracted pneumonia. Propped up on pillows, he was happily conducting an imaginary orchestra when the baton dropped from his lifeless fingers, and he fell back, dead. "Thus departed Hiawatha, Hiawatha, the beloved," greatest composer of his own race, and worthy of a place among great composers of any race.

George Gershwin

"GLORIFIER OF AMERICAN JAZZ"

[*Born September 26, 1898—*   ]

A N APPARENTLY ordinary little boy was born to a wholly ordinary Brooklyn family September 26, 1898, and pursued his uneventful way through public school, a roller skating champion wholly innocent of music other than the clatter of dishes in his father's restaurant.

A secondhand upright piano, acquired for his brother Ira, so fascinated him that the lessons destined for Ira were administered to George, with the result that when he played his star piece for a new teacher, Jay Hambitzer, that gentleman exclaimed "My God, who taught you that stuff? Let's go kill him right now." Four years with Hambitzer, and constant study through intensive listening, made a real pianist of George.

Since the columns of figures at the High School of Commerce could not compete with the rows of notes in his restless mind, he left school at sixteen to become a "plugger" at Remick's, the music publishers, a bit of Tin Pan Alley experience such as "made" Jerome Kern and Irving Berlin. From playing other people's music to writing his own came naturally. On salary with Harms, he wrote his first musical comedy success, *La La Lucille*, and his first song hit, *The Suanee*. From then on, life was a succession of hits,—*Primrose*, *Lady Be Good*, *Funny Face*, *Rosalie*, with his brother Ira playing a witty Gilbert to George's lyric Sullivan. *An American in Paris*, a comedy of homesickness inspired by his first trip abroad, was an outstanding success, and affluence for the Gershwin family followed as the night the day.

In 1922 Eva Gauthier dared to put a group of George's jazz songs on a recital program. Two years later his *Rhapsody in Blue* lifted him bodily into the ranks of serious composers. Since his first performance of the piano part with the Whiteman orchestra he has played it all over Europe, and everywhere it is hailed as a true expression of one aspect of twentieth century America. Fresh, melodious, original. it presents jazz for the first time as a thing of beauty, as well as wit.

He never played a piano concerto until he wrote one, but in his *Concerto in F*, *Piano Preludes*, and *Rhapsody in Rivets* he continued along the new path he had opened. With him, as one critic remarked, jazz is not a trick, it is a quality. He is studying harmony and counterpoint with the ambition of writing symphonies, operas, chamber music, concertos, all the old forms in the new American idiom which he has made peculiarly his own.

Bibliography

GENERAL REFERENCE BOOKS

APPRECIATION—

Elson, Arthur—*Book of Musical Knowledge*—HM—1915
Krehbiel, Edward—*How to Listen to Music*—CSS—1896
Moore, Douglas—*Listening to Music*—WWN—1932
Surette & Mason—*Appreciation of Music*—BT—1908

BIOGRAPHY—

Bridge, Frederick—*Twelve Good Musicians*—KPTT
Brower, Harriette—*Story Lives of Master Musicians*—FAS—1922
Chantavoine, Jean—*De Couperin à Debussy*—FA—1921
Chapin, Anna Alice—*Masters of Music*—DM—1901
Clément, Felix—*Musiciens Célèbres*—Hachette—1878
Dole, Nathan Haskell—*Famous Composers*—TYC—1891
Downes, Olin—*The Lure of Music*—H—1918
Engel, Carl—*Alla Breve: From Bach to Debussy*—GS
Fuller-Maitland, H.—*Masters of German Music*—London—1894
Hadow, Sir Henry—*Studies in Modern Music*—M—1892
Hargrave, Mary—*Earlier French Musicians*—KPTT
Huneker, James G.—*Mezzo-Tints in Modern Music*—CSS—1905
Isaacson, Charles D.—*Face to Face with Great Musicians*—BL—1918
Little Biographies Series—BH—1925
Mason, Daniel Gregory—*The Romantic Composers*—M
Mason, Daniel Gregory—*Contemporary Composers*—M—1926
Masters of Music Series—BG—Boston—1903-7
Montagu-Nathan, M.—*Contemporary Russian Composers*—FAS
Rolland, Romain—*Musicians of To-day*—HH—1917
Rolland, Romain—*Some Musicians of Former Days*—HH—1915
Rosenfeld, Paul—*Musical Portraits*—HB—1920
Sabayaneff, Leonid—*Modern Russian Composers*—I—1917
Schwimmer, Franziska—*Great Musicians as Children*—DD—1929
Streatfield, R. A.—*Life Stories of Great Composers*—P—1910
Streatfield, R. H.—*Masters of Italian Music*—CSS—1895
Streatfield, R. A.—*Modern Music & Musicians*—Meth—1906
Upton, George P.—*Standard Musical Biographies*—ACM—1910
Willeby, Charles—*Masters of English Music*—OM—1897

ESSAYS—

Fraser, Andrew A.—*Essays on Music*—O—1930
Gilman, Lawrence—*Aspects of Modern Opera*—JL—1909
Gilman, Lawrence—*The Music of To-morrow*—JL—1907
Gilman, Lawrence—*Phases of Modern Music*—H—1904
Hadow, Henry—*Collected Essays*—O—1928
Howard, John Tasker—*Our American Music*—TYC—1930
Huneker, James—*Overtones*—CSS—1904
Huneker, James—*Ivory, Apes & Peacocks*—CSS—1915
Marliave, Joseph de—*Etudes Musicales*
Mason, Daniel Gregory—*The Dilemma of American Music*—M—1928
Mason, Daniel Gregory—*Tune In, America*—AK—1931
Van Vechten, Carl—*In the Garret*—AK—1920
Van Vechten, Carl—*Music After the Great War*—GS—1915

HISTORY—

Aubry, Jean—*La Musique Française d'Aujourd'hui*—P&Cie—1916
Bauer & Peyser—*How Music Grew*—GPP—1925
Bekker, Paul—*The Story of Music*—WWN—1927
Clément, Felix—*Histoire de la Musique*
Coeuroy, André—*La Musique Française Moderne*—D—1922
Dickinson—*The Study of the History of Music*—CSS—1926
Gray, Cecil—*History of Music*—KPTT
Gray, Cecil—*A Survey of Contemporary Music*—O—1924
Hawkins, Sir John—*General History of the Science & Practice of Music*—TP—London—1776
Henderson, W. J.—*The Story of Music*—LG—1889
Hill, E. B.—*Modern French Music*—HM—1924
Krehbiel, H. E.—*A Book of Operas*—M—1909
Laloy, Louis—*La Musique Retrouvée*—Plon—1928
Mason, Daniel Gregory—*Beethoven and His Fore-Runners*—M—1904
Parry, Sir Hubert—*Evolution of the Art of Music*—A—1896
Pratt, Waldo Selden—*History of Music*—GS—1927
Poueigh, Jean—*Musiciens Français d'Aujourd'hui*—MF—1928
Weingartner, Felix—*The Symphony Since Beethoven*—OD—1904
Whitcomb, I. M.—*Young People's Story of Music*—DM—1921
Wilm, Grace—*History of Music*—DM—1930

ENCYCLOPEDIAS—

Encyclopedia Britannica
Grove, Sir George—*Dictionary of Music & Musicians*—M
Hull, A. E.—*Dictionary of Modern Music & Musicians*—Dent—1924
Oxford History of Music—O
Pratt, Waldo Selden—*New Encyclopedia of Music & Musicians*—M—1924

PERIODICALS—

Poole's Index for Magazine Articles
British Musician—London
Chesterian—London
Musical Times—London
Musical Opinion—London
Musical Standard—London
Musical America—New York
Musical Courier—New York
Musical Leader—New York
Musical Quarterly—New York
Musik—Berlin
Monthly Musical Record—London
La Revue Musicale—Paris
The Sackbut—London
Program Notes of the Boston Symphony Concerts, edited by Philip Hale
Program Notes of the Philharmonic Society of New York, by Lawrence Gilman

PERSONAL REFERENCE BOOKS

PERSONAL REFERENCES—

Collet, Henri—*Albeniz et Granados*—FA
Forkel—*Johann Sebastian Bach*—HB—1920
Terry, Charles S.—*Bach*—O—1928
Schweitzer—*J. S. Bach*—M
Speria—*J. S. Bach*—NOV—London—1884
Bekker, Paul—*Beethoven*—Dent—1912

Goss, Madeleine—*Beethoven*—DD—1932
Rolland, Romain—*Beethoven*—KPTT—1927
Thayer, Alexander Wheelock—*Beethoven*—BA—1921
Berlioz, (tr. Boult, K.)—*Life of Hector Berlioz*—DU—1903
Parker, D. C.—*Bizet*—KPTT—1926
Malfatti—(I) *Luigi Boccherini*—Lucca—1905
Abraham, Gerald E.—*Borodin*—WR—London
Fuller-Maitland, J. A.—*Johannes Brahms*—METH—1911

Pulver, Jeffrey—*Brahms*—KPTT—1926
Specht, Richard—*Brahms*—Dent—1930
Lee, C. M.—*Brahms*—CSS—1916
Decsey, Ernest—(G) *Bruckner*—SL—1919
Fellowes, Edmund H.—*William Byrd*—O—1923
Howe, Frank—*William Byrd*—DU—1928
Bellasis, Edward—*Cherubini*—BO—London—1874
Niecks, Frederick—*Chopin*—NOV—1904
Huneker, James—*Chopin, the Man and His Music*—CSS—1910
Strachey, M.—*The Nightingale* (Chopin)—LG—1925
Tiersot, Julien—*Les Couperin*—FA—1926
Daly, Wm. H.—*Debussy*—1908
Laloy, Louis (F)—*Debussy*—1909
Lepine, Jean (F)—*La Vie de Claude Debussy*—Al—1930
Donati-Petteni, G.—*Donizetti* (I)—FF—1930
Hoffmeister, Karel—*Dvořák*—JL—1928
Newman, Ernest—*Elgar*—BR—1906
Porte, J. F.—*Sir Edward Elgar*—DU—1921
Trench, J. B.—*de Falla and Spanish Music*—AK—1929
Milligan, Harold Vincent—*Stephen Collins Foster*—GS—1920
d'Indy, Vincent—*César Franck*—JL—1910
Goldberg, Isaac—*George Gershwin*—SS—1931
Newman, Ernest—*Gluck and the Opera*—DOB—1895
Dorscher, Georg (G)—*Gluck*—1918
Gounod (tr. Hutchinson)—*Reminiscences*—WH—1896
Finck, Henry T.—*Grieg and His Music*—DM—1929
Brenet, Michael—*Haydn*—O—1926
Cowen, Sir Frederick—*Haydn*—FAS—1912
Hadden, J. C.—*Haydn*—Dent, London—1902
Hadow, W. H.—*A Croatian Composer* (Haydn)—SE—1897
Davey, Henry—*Handel*—FAS—1913
Flower, Newman—*Handel*—CA—1923
Rolland, Romain—*Handel*—KPTT—1916
Streatfield, R. A.—*Handel*—Meth—1909
Kaye, Joseph—*Victor Herbert*—Watt—1931
Borgex, Louis (F)—*Vincent d'Indy*—DUR—1913
Hervey, Arthur—*Franz Liszt*—JL—1911
Huneker, James—*Franz Liszt*—CSS—1911
Prunières, Henry—*Lully*—Laurens
Gilman, Lawrence—*Edward MacDowell*—JL—1906
Specht, Richard (G)—*Gustav Mahler*—SL—1918
Stefan, Paul (G)—*Gustav Mahler*—GS
Bastianelli, Giannotto (I)—*Pietro Mascagni*—RR—1910
Finck, Henry T.—*Massenet and His Operas*—JL—1910
Massenet, Jules—*Souvenirs* (tr.)—SM—1919
Moschelers—*Letters of Mendelssohn* (tr.)—Ti—1888
Stratton, Stephen S.—*Mendelssohn*—DU—1901

Prunières, Henry—*Monteverdi*—DU
Dent—*Mozart and His Operas*—CH
Hussey, D.—*Mozart*—KPTT—1928
Calvacoressi, Michel—*Musorgsky*—DU—1920
Raugel, Felix—*Palestrina*—REN—1930
Adami (tr. Makin)—*Letters of Puccini*—Lip—1931
Dry Wakeling—*Puccini*—JL—1896
Arundell, Denis—*Henry Purcell*—O—1927
Cummings, Wm. H.—*Purcell*—CSS—1881
Laloy, Louis (F)—*Rameau*—FA—1909
Manuel, Roland—*Maurice Ravel*—1928
Montagu-Nathan, M.—*Rimsky-Korsakoff*—DUF—1917
Rimsky-Korsakoff—*My Musical Life*—AK—1923
Cowen, Sir Frederic—*Rossini*—FAS—1912
Stendhal—*Memoirs of Rossini*—Ho—1824
M'Arthur, A.—*Anton Rubinstein*—AB—1889
Saint-Saëns—*Musical Memories*—SM—1919
Dent, E. J.—*Allessandro Scarlatti*—ARN—1905
Wellesz, Egon—*Arnold Schoenberg*—DU—1925
Ewen, David—*The Unfinished Symphony, A Story Life of Schubert*—MC—1931
Kobald, Karl—*Schubert and His Times*—AK—1929
Whitaker-Wilson, C.—*Franz Schubert*—WR—1928
Basch, Victor (tr. Phillips)—*Schumann, a Life of Suffering*—AK—1931
Bedford, Herbert—*Robert Schumann*—H—1925
Niecks, Frederick—*Robert Schumann*—DU—1925
Njedly, Zdenek—*Frederick Smetana*—Bles—1924
Kobald, Karl—*Johann Strauss*—1925
Engel, Ehrich (G)—*Johann Strauss und Seine Zeit*—1911
Finck, Henry T.—*Richard Strauss, the Man and His Works*—LB
Newman, Ernest—*Richard Strauss*—JL
Schaeffner, André (F)—*Stravinsky*—1931
de Schloezer, Boris (F)—*Igor Stravinsky*—1929
Goldberg, Isaac—*The Story of Gilbert and Sullivan*—SS—1928
Sullivan and Flower—*Sir Arthur Sullivan, His Life, Letters and Diaries*—DD—1927
Berwick-Sayers—*Samuel Coleridge-Taylor*—CA—1915
Evans, Edwin—*Tschaikovsky*—DU—1931
Newmarch, Rosa—*Tschaikovsky*—JL—1900
Pougin, Arthur—*Verdi: An Anecdotic History*—GC—1887
Finck, Henry T.—*Wagner and His Works*—CSS—1893
Gautier, Judith—*Wagner at Home*—MB—1910
Newman, Ernest—*Fact and Fiction about Wagner*—CA—1931
Newman, Ernest—*Wagner as Man and Artist*—AK—1924
Wagner, Richard—*My Life*—CO—1911
von Weber, Max M.—*Carl Maria von Weber*—SCH—1865

A—D. Appleton & Co.; AB—Adam & Black; ACM—A. C. McClurg & Co.; AK—Alfred Knopf; AL—Allin Michel; ARN—Arnold; BA—Beethoven Assn.; BG—Bates & Guild; BH—Breitkopf & Härdel; BL—Boni & Liveright; BO—Burns & Oats; BR—Brentano; BT—Baker & Taylor Co.; CA—Cassell; CH—Chatto & Windus; CO—Constable & Co.; CSS—Charles Scribners' Sons; D—Delagrave; DD—Doubleday Doran; DM—Dodd Mead & Co.; DOB—Dobell & Co.; DU—Dutton; DUF—Duffield & Co.; DUR—Durana et Fils; FA—Felix Alcan; FAS—Frederick A. Stokes & Co.; FT—Fratelli Trèves; GC—Grevel & Co.; GPP—G. P. Putnam & Co.; GS—G. Schirmer; H—Harper Bros.; HB—Harcourt Brace & Co.; HH—Henry Holt & Co.; HM—Houghton Mifflin & Co.; HO—Hookham & Co.; I—International Pub. Co.; JL—John Lane & Co.; KPTT—Kegan, Paul, Trench & Trübner; LB—Little, Brown & Co.; LG—Longmans Green & Co.; LIP—Lippincott; M—Macmillan Company; MB—Miller & Boon; MC—Modern Classics; METH—Methuen; MF—Mercure de France; NOV—Novello & Co.; O—Oxford Univ. Press; OD—Oliver Ditson; OM—Osgood, McIlvaine Co.; P—Presser & Co.; P&Cie—Perrin et Cie; REN—Librairie Renouard; RR—Riccardo Ricciardi; SCH—Simpson, Chapman & Hall; SE—Seeley & Co.; SL—Schuster & Loeffler; SM—Small Maynard & Co.; SS—Simon & Schuster; TI—Tichnor & Co.; TP—T. Payne & Son; TYC—T. Y. Crowell & Co; WH—Wm. Heinemann; WR—Wm. Reeves; WWN—W. W. Norton.